"Dr. Franklin's own excited, uproariously witty reports to his family, his friends, and his scientific colleagues in Europe and America create an incomparable portrait of science in the eighteenth century. Reading these letters fosters a new affection for our country's foremost and most beloved inventor."

—DAVA SOBEL,
author of *Longitude* and *Galileo's Daughter*

"This marvelous collection helps rescue Ben Franklin from our impression of him as a genial tinkerer flying kites in the rain. In fact, he was a serious scientist whose letters reveal the scope of his ideas, ranging from daylight savings time to bifocals to magnetism. This book crackles with his wonderful mental energy."

—WALTER ISAACSON,
managing editor of *Time*

PENNSYLVANIA PAPERBACKS

THE INGENIOUS
Dr.
FRANKLIN

SELECTED SCIENTIFIC LETTERS

OF

BENJAMIN FRANKLIN

Edited by

NATHAN G. GOODMAN

PHILADELPHIA

UNIVERSITY OF PENNSYLVANIA PRESS

Copyright © 1931 University of Pennsylvania Press
All rights reserved
Printed in the United States of America on acid-free paper

10 9 8 7 6 5 4 3 2

Published by
University of Pennsylvania Press
Philadelphia, Pennsylvania 19104-4011

Library of Congress Catalog Card Number 31-34123

ISBN 0-8122-1067-0

CONTENTS

DIVERS EXPERIMENTS AND OBSERVATIONS

SCIENTIFIC DEDUCTIONS AND CONJEC-TURES

PREFACE

THE new Benjamin Franklin Memorial and the Franklin Institute in Philadelphia, emphasizing mechanical skill, is a fitting monument to the ingenious scientist of the eighteenth century. His engaging letters and papers, of a practical, experimental, and conjectural nature, being tucked away in ponderous volumes of Collected Works, and therefore not widely known, are now in these pages made available to the general reader. In our scientific age these letters should be especially alluring.

In his writings Franklin used capitals abundantly and indiscriminately. In the present volume unnecessary capitals have been eliminated, but no alterations have been made in the original spelling and punctuation.

For permission to include in this volume hitherto unpublished letters thanks are due Mr. William Smith Mason, The Rosenbach Company, and the American Philosophical Society. I also owe a debt of gratitude to the many private collectors and librarians who gave me access to their collections of Franklin manuscripts, and to my wife, Julia N. Goodman, for many suggestions.

NATHAN G. GOODMAN

Germantown, Philadelphia
July fourth, 1931

ILLUSTRATIONS

* *Line illustrations redrawn by John S. Detlie from previous editions of Franklin's works.*

THE INGENIOUS
Dr. FRANKLIN

ON his second voyage to England Benjamin Franklin barely escaped shipwreck off Falmouth. In a letter to his wife he reported the occurrence which called forth, as usual, a reaction with a practical slant: "Perhaps I should on this occasion vow to build a chapel to some saint; but . . . if I were to vow at all, it should be to build a lighthouse."

Benjamin Franklin was incredibly curious. He asked more questions than his friends could answer; he demanded the how and the why of the most baffling as well as the commonest phenomena. In his innate curiosity lay the germ of his passion for the practical. When an explanation was neither forthcoming nor satisfactory, he himself set about solving the problem or unraveling the mystery. First he inquired; then he experimented, contriving unique apparatus, and setting up a rational procedure, observing effects minutely, checking results and drawing original conclusions. Although he possessed the eighteenth-century philosophic turn of mind, Franklin was a stride or so ahead of most of his contemporaries, in that abstract solutions alone did not satisfy him. He sought to direct his deductions into utilitarian channels. To bring more comfort and security to his fellow man was the object of his experiments and the intent of his conjectures.

Benjamin Franklin was not only the most inquisitive, but also the most ingenious man in America in the eighteenth century.

He dipped into the fields of physics, meteorology, natural history, geology, chemistry, mechanics, agriculture, medicine, and mathematics. At the same time he was a master printer, successful journalist, distinguished diplomat, and public-spirited citizen. With his name are associated the open stove, improved lamps for street lighting, the lightning rod, bifocals, the public library, and the fire company. He offered practical suggestions on navigation, street paving, street cleaning, police protection, ventilation, and education. In an extensive correspondence he exchanged ideas with the leaders of thought in Europe and in America. One finds letters to such eminent men as Priestley, Cavendish, and Lavoisier on physics and chemistry; to John Bartram on agriculture; to the President of the Royal Society, Sir Joseph Banks, on balloons; and to Dr. Benjamin Rush on medicine.

It was as America's first great electrician that Franklin won his initial laurels as an internationally known scientist. Fascinated by a lecture on electricity which he heard in Boston in 1746, he decided to investigate the subject. From his London friend, Peter Collinson, he received the necessary apparatus; and shortly he proceeded to make demonstrations before the Junto in Philadelphia. Then, in one of the most important letters in the history of electricity, written to Collinson on July 11, 1747, Franklin propounded a new theory of electricity, pointing out for the first time the distinction between positive and negative electric excitement. A few weeks later, in a letter dispatched to Collinson on September 1, we find that Franklin had already made improvements upon the Leyden jar. In 1749 he set forth the single-fluid theory of electricity in an important paper: "Opinions and Conjectures, concerning the Properties and Effects of the Electrical Matter. . . ." His interest in the electrical nature of clouds led to the invention of the lightning rod, still our only means of protection against the terrifying and destructive fire of the heavens. On the foundations laid by Franklin modern theories of electricity have been built.

In a clear and carefully constructed paper, "Aurora Borealis, Suppositions and Conjectures towards forming an Hypothesis for its Explanation," Franklin presented his theory of the northern lights, which he probably observed on his voyages to England. The constant circulation of air, caused by varying temperatures, moves the clouds and vapors above the earth. These in turn conduct their electrical charge through the atmosphere. The vast expanses of ice and snow in the polar regions tend to accumulate electricity carried there by the snow and moisture, the resultant overcharging giving rise to the aurora. Franklin sums up his theory:

> May not then the great quantity of electricity brought into the polar regions by the clouds, which are condens'd there, and fall in snow, which electricity would enter the earth, but cannot penetrate the ice; may it not, I say (*as a bottle overcharged*) break thro' that low atmosphere and run along in the vacuum over the air towards the equator, diverging as the degrees of longitude enlarge, strongly visible where densest, and becoming less visible as it more diverges; till it finds a passage to the earth in more temperate climates, or is mingled with the upper air?

In a particularly fine letter to the Abbé Soulavie, September 22, 1782, Franklin gives reign to his fancy in conjecturing upon the structure and formation of the earth. His suppositions are striking, inasmuch as opportunity for exhaustive observation and study was not within his power.

Franklin's interest in mechanics was early manifested when, as a young man, he worked in a printing shop. He experimented constantly. Whenever possible, he tried designs of his own invention. "Our printing house often wanted sorts" [loose type for making corrections], he tells us in the Autobiography, "and there was no letter founder in America . . . I now contrived a mould, made use of the letters we had as puncheons, struck the matrices in lead, and thus supply'd in a pretty tolerable way all deficiencies." And later he contrived the first copper-plate press in America.

In his first years as a printer Franklin observed that, although the colonists were thirsty for news, little attention was paid to organized news service. Gossip there was at the inns and taverns where, before the inauguration of an efficient postal service, sailors deposited the mail from Europe. Not infrequently letters were read aloud in the taverns. Sensing the desire for news, Franklin became in turn publisher of *The Pennsylvania Gazette, Poor Richard's Almanack,* the *Philadelphische Zeitung* (the first foreign-language newspaper published in America), and *The General Magazine and Historical Chronicle for all the British Plantations in America.* These papers developed among the colonies a feeling of common purpose.

On his long ocean voyages Franklin's interest shifted from the world of affairs to the mysteries of the sea, sky, and air. He was absorbed with the aspects of the skies, the position of the sun and moon, the changing currents, and the ship's course, recording ideas for the improvement of methods of sailing, and formulating questions which arose in his mind concerning the phenomena he observed. "What is he measuring now?" the Captain would say as he stood with his hands on his hips and watched the star passenger. In a remarkable *Journal of a Voyage from London to Philadelphia* which Franklin kept on a transatlantic voyage, at the age of twenty, he noted the state of the winds, a rainbow, an eclipse of the sun. On his very last voyage back to America from Europe, at the age of seventy-nine, although he was in poor health, he wrote at length on the construction and provisioning of ships, the winds, the currents, and the temperature of the seas. "I think a set of experiments might be instituted," he suggested, "first to determine the most proper form of the hull for swift sailing; next, the best dimensions and most proper place for the masts; then the form and quantity of sails and their position, as the winds may be."

Once a thermometer, sent to Franklin from London, reached Philadelphia broken. He tells us how he tried to repair it:

I got a thin copper ball nicely made, and fix'd to the tube with a screw plug entering the ball at the bottom, by means of which screw going into the cavity of the ball, more or less, among the mercury, I hoped to lessen or enlarge the space at pleasure, and by that means find the true quantity of mercury it ought to contain to rise and fall exactly with the others in the same temperature of air.

Franklin invented his famous stove in 1742. To honor the inventor, the Governor of Pennsylvania proposed that he be given a monopoly on the sale of the stoves. Franklin, however, refused to accept this favor, believing "that as we enjoy great advantages from the inventions of others, we should be glad of an opportunity to serve others by any invention of ours, and this we should do freely and generously." In order to promote the

[5]

use of the stoves, Franklin published a pamphlet in which he discussed their methods of construction and operation, suggesting that "you do not lose the pleasing sight nor use of the fire, as in the Dutch stoves, but may boil the tea-kettle, warm the flat irons, heat heaters, keep warm a dish of victuals by setting it on the top." Franklin gave considerable thought to the construction of chimneys and in a lengthy and illuminating paper addressed to Jan Ingenhousz, August 28, 1785, he answered the question: "What is it then which makes a *smoky chimney;* that is, a chimney which, instead of conveying up all the smoke, discharges a part of it into the room, offending the eyes and damaging the furniture?" In this analysis of "The Causes and Cure of Smoky Chimneys" nine causes are discussed and remedies offered.

The early Americans were glad enough to enjoy the "pleasing sight" of their fires indoors in the evening since the city streets were dark, lonely, and forbidding. Thieves and bandits often lurked in doorways and alleys. The old London globe lamps, occasionally used along the city streets, furnished but little light. Though Franklin was not the first to propose a scheme of street-lighting, he materially improved the old London globes. He designed a lamp

of four flat panes, with a funnel above to draw up the smoke, and crevices admitting air below, to facilitate the ascent of the smoke; by this means they were kept clean and did not grow dark in a few hours, as the London lamps do, but continued bright till morning; and an accidental stroke would generally break but a single pane, easily repair'd.

Reproductions of the Franklin lamp are in use today around Independence Hall in Philadelphia.

To make the streets even safer at night Franklin proposed an organized watch, "the hiring of proper men to serve constantly in that business; and as a more equitable way of supporting the charge, the levying a tax that should be proportion'd to the property."

What of the city during the day? "Mud up to the ankles again!" thundered the apothecary after crossing High Street. Annoyed by the condition of the streets, Franklin harangued the citizens until at length Philadelphia's old High Street (now Market Street) was paved with stone. In 1757 he introduced in the Assembly of his colony a bill providing for the paving of the streets of Philadelphia.

Complaints about the mud and dust, even on the paved streets, continued to be heard. Franklin once more held forth to shopkeepers and housewives, and then, "After some inquiry," he recorded, "I found a poor, industrious man, who was willing to undertake keeping the pavement clean by sweeping it twice a week, carrying off the dirt from before the neighbors' doors, for the sum of sixpence per month, to be paid by each house." While in London he suggested that during the summer months the streets be cleaned in the early morning hours "before the shops and windows of houses are usually opened, when scavengers with close-covered carts shall also carry it away."

The fire hazard in colonial America was great because wood was employed extensively in building construction. There was the ever-present danger of overheated chimneys and of sparks from open fireplaces. Moreover, there was no water-supply system. Franklin was the first man in America to advocate an organization for protection against fire. Thirty Philadelphians agreed to join his Union Fire Company.

Our articles of agreement [detailed Franklin], oblig'd every member to keep always in good order, and fit for use, a certain number of leather buckets, with strong bags and baskets (for packing and transporting of goods), which were to be brought to every fire; and we agreed to meet once a month and spend a social evening together, in discoursing and communicating such ideas as occurred to us upon the subject of fires, as might be useful in our conduct on such occasions.

The idea spread and before long other companies were organized.

Fireproof construction also attracted Franklin's attention. Writing to Samuel Rhoads, June 26, 1770, he said:

It appears to me of great importance to build our dwelling-houses, if we can, in a manner more secure from danger from fire. We scarce ever hear of a fire in Paris. When I was there, I took particular notice of the construction of their houses; and I did not see how one of them could well be burnt. The roofs are slate or tile; the walls are stone; the rooms generally lin'd with stucco or plaister instead of wainscot; the floors of stucco, or of six-square tiles painted brown; or of flag stone, or marble; if any floor were of wood, it was oak wood, which is not so inflammable as pine.

Franklin's practical schemes transcended mere creature comfort in their aims. Philadelphians could sit at ease and improve their minds in the first public library in America, another Franklin "first." "This was the mother of all the North American subscription libraries, now so numerous," commented Franklin in the *Autobiography*. "These libraries have improved the general conversation of the Americans, made the common tradesmen and farmers as intelligent as most gentlemen from other countries, and perhaps have contributed in some degree to the stand so generally made throughout the colonies in defence of their privileges." This defence refers to the War for Independence.

It can be imagined that the room of the first library was well ventilated because the founder was an ardent believer in the value of fresh air. When in London, Franklin was asked to present ideas on a new ventilating system for the House of Commons. Later, in a letter to a correspondent, he wrote: "I now look upon fresh air as a friend; I even sleep with an open window. I am persuaded, that no common air from without is so unwholesome, as the air within a close room, that has been often breath'd and not changed."

With his weak eyes Franklin saw more than many men with strong eyes. As he grew older, he was faced with the necessity of using two pairs of spectacles. He carried in his pocket a special pair for reading. One day he appeared with a most unusual pair of glasses upon which his friends immediately commented. To use two pairs of spectacles was troublesome and he had solved the problem by grinding the first pair of bifocals.

I had formerly two pair of spectacles [he explained], which I shifted occasionally, as in travelling I sometimes read, and often wanted to regard the prospects. Finding this change troublesome, and not always sufficiently ready, I had the glasses cut, and half of each kind associated in the same circle. By this means, as I wear my spectacles constantly, I have only to move my eyes up or down, as I want to see distinctly far or near, the proper glasses being always ready.

In the field of learning and formal education Franklin was interested primarily in practical instruction. His *Proposals Relating to the Education of Youth in Pensilvania* was distributed to the influential men of Pennsylvania in 1749, with the hope that "some publick spirited Gentlemen" would provide the financial support necessary to establish an academy for the youth of the Province. He emphasized the knowledge of one's native tongue rather than an overdose of Latin and Greek. He advocated training in scientific farming as he conceived it, and a thorough course in the history of commerce. The academy, organized in 1749, ultimately became the University of Pennsylvania. For theoretical discussions Franklin founded a Philosophical Society which became the American Philosophical Society.

For a time French and English men of science and learning disregarded Franklin's contributions. They laughed at his experiment with the famous kite for "procuring lightning from the clouds by a pointed rod." To them he sounded like a small boy who had been flying a kite and then had had dreams. Soon, however, Franklin's lightning rod was hailed as a great invention. Other electrical discoveries brought world-wide reputation to Franklin's name. The British scientist, Professor J. J. Thomson, once wrote: "We shall, I am sure, be struck by the similarity between some of the views which we are led to take by the results of the most recent researches, with those enunciated by Franklin in the very infancy of the subject." And many years ago Lord Brougham offered this compliment: "He could make an experiment with less apparatus and conduct his experimental inquiry to a discovery with more ordinary materials than any other philosopher we ever saw. With an old key, a silk thread, some sealing wax and a sheet of paper he discovered the identity of lightning and electricity."

Franklin knew that light-colored shirts are cooler in the summer than dark-colored shirts. How is color related to heat? he asked himself. In a simple experiment in which little squares of different-colored cloth were placed on snow on a sunshiny morning he demonstrated the relationship, and discussed the conclusions in a charming letter to Polly Stevenson:

May we not learn from hence, that black clothes are not so fit to wear in a hot sunny climate or season as white ones, because in such clothes, the body is more heated by the sun when we walk abroad, and are at the same time heated by the exercise, which double heat is apt to bring on putrid dangerous fevers? That summer hats, for men and women, should be white as repelling that heat which gives headaches to many, and to some the fatal stroke that the French call *Coup de Soleil?* That the ladies summer hats, however, should be lined with black, as not reverberating on their faces those rays which are reflected upwards from the earth or water? That the putting a white cap of paper or linnen *within* the crown of a black hat, as some do, will not keep out the heat, tho' it would if placed *without?* That fruit-walls being black'd may receive so much heat from the sun in the daytime, as to continue warm in some degree thro' the night, and thereby preserve the fruit from frosts, or forward its growth?

Nothing escaped Franklin's ever-curious eyes. Some common flies had drowned in a bottle of Madeira wine. Are they really dead? he wondered. In a letter to a French physician he told the story which reads like a student's laboratory experiment.

At the opening of one of the bottles, [he went on], three drowned flies fell into the first glass that was filled. Having heard it remarked that drowned flies were capable of being revived by the rays of the sun, I proposed making the experiment upon these; they were therefore exposed to the sun upon a sieve, which had been employed to strain them out of the wine. In less than three hours, two of them began by degrees to recover life. They commenced by some convulsive motions of the thighs, and at length they raised themselves upon their legs, wiped their eyes with their fore feet, beat and brushed their wings with their hind feet, and soon after began to fly, finding themselves in Old England, without knowing how they came thither. The third continued lifeless till sunset, when, losing all hopes of him, he was thrown away.

With his usual foresight Franklin predicted a great future

for science. He could see airplanes in the future, scientific farming, and preventive medicine. He himself believed that he had been born too soon. He wrote Joseph Priestley that

the rapid progress *true* science now makes, occasions my regretting sometimes that I was born too soon. It is impossible to imagine the height to which may be carried, in a thousand years, the power of man over matter. We may perhaps learn to deprive large masses of their gravity, and give them absolute levity, for the sake of easy transport. Agriculture may diminish its labour and double its produce, all diseases may by sure means be prevented or cured, not excepting even that of Old Age, and our lives lengthened at pleasure even beyond the antediluvian standard.

Franklin realized that many so-called practical schemes prove highly impractical when put to the test. In *Poor Richard's Almanack* for 1757 one finds a satire of rare humor upon the creative genius of many would-be inventors and promoters of private and public projects. It reads:

How to make a STRIKING SUNDIAL, by which not only a man's own family, but all his neighbours for ten miles round, may know what a clock it is, when the sun shines, without seeing the dial.

Chuse an open place in your yard or garden, on which the sun may shine all day without any impediment from trees or buildings. On the ground make out your hour lines, as for a horizontal dial, according to art, taking room enough for the guns. On the line for one o'clock, place one gun; on the two o'clock line two guns, and so of the rest. The guns must all be charged with powder, but ball is unnecessary. Your gnomon or style must have twelve burning glasses annex't to it, and be so placed that the sun shining through the glasses, one after the other, shall cause the focus or burning spot to fall on the hour line of one, for example, at one a clock, and there kindle a train of gunpowder that shall fire one gun. At two a clock, a focus shall fall on the hour line of two, and kindle another train that shall discharge two guns successively: and so of the rest.

Note, there must be 78 guns in all. Thirty-two pounders will be best for this use; but 18 pounders may do, and will cost less, as well as use less powder, for nine pounds of powder will do for one charge of each eighteen pounder, whereas the thirty-two pounders would require for each gun 16 pounds.

Note also, that the chief expense will be the powder, for the cannon once bought, will, with care, last 100 years.

Note moreover, that there will be a great saving of powder in cloudy days.

Kind reader, methinks I hear thee say, that is indeed a good thing to know how the time passes, but this kind of dial, notwithstanding the mentioned savings, would be very expensive; and the cost greater than the advantage, thou art wise, my friend, to be so considerate beforehand; some fools would not have found out so much, till they had made the dial and try'd it. . . . Let all such learn that many a private and many a publick project, are like this striking dial, great cost for little profit.

Harassed by affairs of state, perplexed by the mysteries of the universe, challenged by the needs of his fellow man, Franklin developed a vigorous personality which survives to this day by virtue of its magnetism, its humanity, and its amazing wisdom.

PRACTICAL SCHEMES
and SUGGESTIONS

DAYLIGHT SAVING

To the Authors of
The Journal of Paris

[1784]

MESSIEURS,

YOU often entertain us with accounts of new discoveries. Permit me to communicate to the public, through your paper, one that has lately been made by myself, and which I conceive may be of great utility.

I was the other evening in a grand company, where the new lamp of Messrs. Quinquet and Lange was introduced, and much admired for its splendour; but a general inquiry was made, whether the oil it consumed was not in proportion to the light it afforded, in which case there would be no saving in the use of it. No one present could satisfy us in that point, which all agreed ought to be known, it being a very desirable thing to lessen, if possible, the expense of lighting our apartments, when every other article of family expense was so much augmented.

I was pleased to see this general concern for economy, for I love economy exceedingly.

I went home, and to bed, three or four hours after midnight, with my head full of the subject. An accidental sudden noise waked me about six in the morning, when I was surprised to find my room filled with light; and I imagined at first, that a number of those lamps had been brought into it; but, rubbing my eyes, I perceived the light came in at the windows. I got up and looked out to see what might be the occasion of it, when I saw the sun just rising above the horizon, from whence he poured his rays plentifully into my chamber, my domestic having negligently omitted, the preceding evening, to close the shutters.

I looked at my watch, which goes very well, and found that it was but six o'clock; and still thinking it something extraordinary that the sun should rise so early, I looked into the almanac, where I found it to be the hour given for his rising on that day. I looked forward, too, and found he was to rise still earlier every day till towards the end of June; and that at no time in the year he retarded his rising so long as till eight o'clock. Your readers, who with me have never seen any signs of sunshine before noon, and seldom regard the astronomical part of the almanac, will be as much astonished as I was, when they hear of his rising so early; and especially when I assure them, *that he gives light as soon as he rises.* I am convinced of this. I am certain of my fact. One cannot be more certain of any fact. I saw it with my own eyes. And, having repeated this observation the three following mornings, I found always precisely the same result.

Yet it so happens, that when I speak of this discovery to others, I can easily perceive by their countenances, though they forbear expressing it in words, that they do not quite believe me. One, indeed, who is a learned natural philosopher, has assured me that I must certainly be mistaken as to the circumstance of the light coming into my room; for it being well known, as he says, that there could be no light abroad at that hour, it follows that none could enter from without; and that of consequence, my windows being accidentally left open, instead of letting in the light, had only served to let out the darkness; and he used many ingenious arguments to show me how I might, by that means, have been deceived. I owned that he puzzled me a little, but he did not satisfy me; and the subsequent observations I made, as above mentioned, confirmed me in my first opinion.

This event has given rise in my mind to several serious and important reflections. I considered that, if I had not been awakened so early in the morning, I should have slept six hours longer by the light of the sun, and in exchange have lived six hours the following night by candle-light; and, the latter being a much more expensive light than the former, my love of economy induced me to muster up what little arithmetic I was master of, and to make some calculations, which I shall give you, after observing that utility is, in my opinion the test of value in matters of invention, and that a discovery which can be applied to no use, or is not good for something, is good for nothing.

I took for the basis of my calculation the supposition that there are one hundred thousand families in Paris, and that these families consume in the night half a pound of bougies, or candles, per hour. I think this is a moderate allowance, taking one family with another; for though I believe some consume less, I know that many consume a great deal more. Then estimating seven hours per day as the medium quantity between the time of the sun's rising and ours, he rising during the six following months from six to eight hours before noon, and there being seven hours of course per night in which we burn candles, the account will stand thus;—

In the six months between the 20th of March and the 20th of September, there are

Nights 183
Hours of each night in which we burn candles . . . 7

Multiplication gives for the total number of hours . . 1,281
These 1,281 hours multiplied by 100,000, the
number of inhabitants, give 128,100,000
One hundred twenty-eight millions and one
hundred thousand hours, spent at Paris by
candle-light, which, at half a pound of wax
and tallow per hour, gives the weight of . . 64,050,000
Sixty-four millions and fifty thousand of pounds,
which, estimating the whole at the medium
price of thirty sols the pound, makes the sum
of ninety-six millions and seventy-five thousand livres tournois 96,075,000

An immense sum! that the city of Paris might save every year, by the economy of using sunshine instead of candles.

If it should be said, that people are apt to be obstinately attached to old customs, and that it will be difficult to induce them to rise before noon, consequently my discovery can be of little use; I answer, *Nil desperandum.* I believe all who have common sense, as soon as they have learnt from this paper that it is daylight when the sun rises, will contrive to rise with him; and, to compel the rest, I would propose the following regulations;

First. Let a tax be laid of a louis per window, on every window that is provided with shutters to keep out the light of the sun.

Second. Let the same salutary operation of police be made use of, to prevent our burning candles, that inclined us last winter to be more economical in burning wood; that is, let guards be placed in the shops of the wax and tallow chandlers, and no family be permitted to be supplied with more than one pound of candles per week.

Third. Let guards also be posted to stop all the coaches, &c. that would pass the streets after sunset, except those of physicians, surgeons, and midwives.

Fourth. Every morning, as soon as the sun rises, let all the bells in every church be set ringing; and if that is not sufficient, let cannon be fired in every street, to wake the sluggards effectually, and make them open their eyes to see their true interest.

All the difficulty will be in the first two or three days; after which the reformation will be as natural and easy as the present irregularity; for, *ce n'est que le premier pas qui coûte*. Oblige a man to rise at four in the morning, and it is more than probable he will go willingly to bed at eight in the evening; and, having had eight hours sleep, he will rise more willingly at four in the morning following. But this sum of ninety-six millions and seventy-five thousand livres is not the whole of what may be saved by my economical project. You may observe, that I have calculated upon only one half of the year, and much may be saved in the other, though the days are shorter. Besides, the immense stock of wax and tallow left unconsumed during the summer, will probably make candles much cheaper for the ensuing winter, and continue them cheaper as long as the proposed reformation shall be supported.

For the great benefit of this discovery, thus freely communicated and bestowed by me on the public, I demand neither place, pension, exclusive privilege, nor any other reward whatever. I expect only to have the honour of it. And yet I know there are little, envious minds, who will, as usual, deny me this, and say, that my invention was known to the ancients, and perhaps they may bring passages out of the old books in proof of it. I will not dispute with these people, that the ancients knew not the sun would rise at certain hours; they possibly had, as we have, almanacs that predicted it; but it does not follow thence, that they knew *he gave light as soon as he rose.* This is what I claim as my discovery. If the ancients knew it, it might have been long since forgotten; for it certainly was unknown to the moderns, at least to the Parisians, which to prove, I need use but one plain simple argument. They are as well instructed, judicious, and prudent a people as exist anywhere in the world, all professing, like myself, to be lovers of economy; and, from the many heavy taxes required from them by the necessities of the state, have surely an abundant reason to be economical. I say it is impossible that so sensible a people, under such circumstances, should have lived so long by the smoky, unwholesome, and enormously expensive light of candles, if they had really known, that they might have had as much pure light of the sun for nothing. I am, &c.

A SUBSCRIBER.

TREATMENT *for* GOUT

TO

A<small>LEXANDER</small> S<small>MALL</small>

Passy, July 22, 1780.

YOU inquired about my gout, and I forgot to acquaint you, that I had treated it a little cavalierly in its two last accesses. Finding one night that my foot gave me more pain after it was covered warm in bed, I put it out of bed naked; and, perceiving it easier, I let it remain longer than I at first designed, and at length fell asleep leaving it there till morning. The pain did not return, and I grew well. Next winter, having a second attack, I repeated the experiment; not with such immediate success in dismissing the gout, but constantly with the effect of rendering it less painful, so that it permitted me to sleep every night. I should mention, that it was my son who gave me the first intimation of this practice. He being in the old opinion, that the gout was to be drawn out by transpiration; and, having heard me say, that perspiration was carried on more copiously when the body was naked, than when clothed, he put his foot out of bed to increase that discharge, and found ease by it, which he thought a confirmation of the doctrine. But this method requires to be confirmed by more experiments, before one can conscientiously recommend it. I give it you, however, in exchange for your receipt of tartar emetic; because the commerce of philosophy as well as other commerce, is best promoted by taking care to make returns. I am ever yours most affectionately,

B. FRANKLIN.

COLD AIR BATH

TO

BARBEU DUBOURG

London, July 28, 1768.

I GREATLY approve the epithet which you give, in your letter of the 8th of June, to the new method of treating the small-pox, which you call the *tonic* or bracing method; I will take occasion from it to mention a practice to which I have accustomed myself. You know the cold bath has long been in vogue here as a tonic; but the shock of the cold water has always appeared to me, generally speaking, as too violent, and I have found it much more agreeable to my constitution to bathe in another element, I mean cold air. With this view I rise almost every morning, and sit in my chamber without any clothes whatever, half an hour or an hour, according to the season, either reading or writing. This practice is not in the least painful, but, on the contrary, agreeable; and, if I return to bed afterwards, before I dress myself, as sometimes happens, I make a supplement to my night's rest of one or two hours of the most pleasing sleep that can be imagined. I find no ill consequences whatever resulting from it, and that at least it does not injure my health, if it does not in fact contribute much to its preservation. I shall therefore call it for the future a *bracing* or *tonic* bath.

B. FRANKLIN.

ELECTRICAL TREATMENT
for PARALYSIS

TO

JOHN PRINGLE

Craven-Street, Dec. 21, 1757.

SIR,

IN compliance with your request, I send you the following account of what I can at present recollect relating to the effects of electricity in paralytic cases, which have fallen under my observation.

Some years since, when the news-papers made mention of great cures performed in *Italy* and *Germany*, by means of electricity, a number of paralytics, were brought to me from different parts of *Pensylvania,* and the neighboring provinces, to be electrised, which I did for them at their request. My method was, to place the patient first in a chair, on an electric stool, and draw a number of large strong sparks from all parts of the affected limb or side. Then I fully charged two six gallon glass jars, each of which had about three square feet of surface coated; and I sent the united shock of these through the affected limb or limbs, repeating the stroke commonly three times each day. The first thing observed, was an immediate greater sensible warmth in the lame limbs that had received the stroke, than in the others; and the next morning the patients usually related, that they had in the night felt a pricking sensation in the flesh of the paralytic limbs; and would sometimes shew a number of small red spots, which they supposed were occasioned by those prickings. The limbs, too, were found more capable of voluntary motion, and seemed to receive strength. A man, for instance, who could not the first day lift the lame hand from off his knee, would the next day raise it four or five inches, the third day higher; and on the fifth day was able, but with a feeble languid motion, to take off his hat. These appearances gave great spirits to the patients, and made them hope a perfect cure; but I do not remember that I ever saw any amendment after the fifth day; which the patients perceiving, and finding the shocks pretty severe, they became discouraged, went home, and in a short time relapsed; so that I never knew any advantage from electricity in palsies that was permanent. And how far the apparent temporary advantage might arise from the exercise in the patients' journey, and coming daily to my house, or from the spirits given by the hope of success, enabling them to exert more strength in moving their limbs, I will not pretend to say.

Perhaps some permanent advantage might have been obtained, if the electric shocks had been accompanied with proper medicine and regimen, under the direction of a skilful physician. It may be, too, that a few great strokes, as given in my method, may not be so proper as many small ones; since, by the account from *Scotland* of a case, in which two hundred shocks from a phial were given daily, it seems, that a perfect cure has been made. As to any uncommon strength supposed to be in the machine used in that case, I imagine it could have no share in the effect produced; since the strength of the shock from charged glass is in proportion to the quantity of surface of the glass coated; so that my shocks from those large jars must have been much greater than any that could be received from a phial held in the hand. I am, with great respect, Sir,

Your most obedient servant,

B. FRANKLIN.

LEAD POISONING

TO

BENJAMIN VAUGHAN

Philada, July 31, 1786.

DEAR FRIEND,

I RECOLLECT, that, when I had the great pleasure of seeing you at Southampton, now a 12month since, we had some conversation on the bad effects of lead taken inwardly; and that at your request I promis'd to send you in writing a particular account of several facts I then mention'd to you, of which you thought some good use might be made. I now sit down to fulfil that promise.

The first thing I remember of this kind was a general discourse in Boston, when I was a boy, of a complaint from North Carolina against New England rum, that it poison'd their people, giving them the dry bellyach, with a loss of the use of their limbs. The distilleries being examin'd on the occasion, it was found that several of them used leaden still-heads and worms, and the physicians were of opinion, that the mischief was occasioned by that use of lead. The legislature of the Massachusetts thereupon pass'd an Act, prohibiting under severe penalties the use of such still-heads and worms thereafter. Inclos'd I send you a copy of the Acct, taken from my printed law-book.

In 1724, being in London, I went to work in the printing-house of Mr. Palmer, Bartholomew Close, as a compositor. I there found a practice, I had never seen before, of drying a case of types (which are wet in distribution) by placing it sloping before the fire. I found this had the additional advantage, when the types were not only dry'd but heated, of being comfortable to the hands working over them in cold weather. I therefore sometimes heated my case when the types did not want drying. But an old workman, observing it, advis'd me not to do so, telling me I might lose the use of my hands by it, as two of our companions had nearly done, one of whom that us'd to earn his guinea a week, could not then make more than ten shillings, and the other, who had the dangles, but seven and sixpence. This, with a kind of obscure pain, that I had sometimes felt, as it were in the bones of my hand when working over the types made very hot, induced me to omit the practice. But talking afterwards with Mr. James, a letter-founder in the same Close, and asking him if his people, who work'd over the little furnaces of melted metal, were not subject to that disorder; he made light of any danger from the effluvia, but ascribed it to particles of the metal swallow'd with their food by slovenly workmen, who went to their meals after handling the metal, without well washing their fingers, so that some of the metalline particles were taken off by their bread and eaten with it. This appeared to have some reason in it. But the pain I had experienc'd made me still afraid of those effluvia.

Being in Derbishire at some of the furnaces for smelting of lead ore, I was told, that the smoke of those furnaces was pernicious to the neighbouring grass and other vegetables; but I do not recollect to have heard any thing of the effect of such vegetables eaten by animals. It may be well to make the enquiry.

In America I have often observ'd, that on the roofs of our shingled houses, where moss is apt to grow in northern exposures, if there be any thing on the roof painted with white lead, such as balusters, or frames of dormant windows, &c., there is constantly a streak on the shingles from such paint down to the eaves, on which no moss will grow, but the wood remains constantly clean and free from it. We seldom drink rain water that falls on our houses; and if we did, perhaps the small quantity of lead, descending from such paint, might not be sufficient to produce any sensible ill effect on our bodies. But I have been told of a case in Europe, I forgot the place, where a whole family was afflicted with what we call the dry bellyach, or *Colica Pictonum*, by drinking rain-water. It was at a country-seat, which, being situated too high to have the advantage of a well, was supply'd with water from a tank, which received the water from the leaded roofs. This had been drunk several years without mischief; but some young trees planted near the house growing up above the roof, and shedding their leaves upon it, it was suppos'd that an acid in those leaves had corroded the lead they cover'd and furnish'd the water of that year with its baneful particles and qualities.

When I was in Paris with Sir John Pringle in 1767, he visited *La Charité*, a hospital particularly famous for the cure of that malady, and brought from thence a pamphlet containing a list of the names of persons, specifying their professions or trades, who had been cured there. I had the curiosity to examine that list, and found that all the patients were of trades, that, some way or other, use or work in lead; such as plumbers, glaziers, painters, &c., excepting only two kinds, stonecutters and soldiers. These I could not reconcile to my notion, that lead was the cause of that disorder. But on my mentioning this difficulty to a physician of that hospital, he inform'd me that the stonecutters are continually using melted lead to fix the ends of iron balustrades in stone; and that the soldiers had been employ'd by painters, as labourers, in grinding of colours.

This, my dear friend, is all I can at present recollect on the subject. You will see by it, that the opinion of this mischievous effect from lead is at least above sixty years old; and you will observe with concern how long a useful truth may be known and exist, before it is generally receiv'd and practis'd on.

I am, ever, yours most effectionately,

B. FRANKLIN.

RULES OF HEALTH AND LONG LIFE

EAT and drink such an exact quantity as the constitution of thy body allows of, in reference to the services of the mind.

They that study much, ought not to eat so much as those that work hard, their digestion being not so good.

The exact quantity and quality, being found out, is to be kept to constantly.

Excess in all other things whatever, as well as in meat and drink, is also to be avoided.

Youth, age, and sick, require a different quantity.

And so do those of contrary complexions; for that which is too much for a phlegmatick man, is not sufficient for a cholerick.

The measure of food ought to be (as much as possibly may be) exactly proportionable to the quality and condition of the stomach, because the stomach digests it.

That quantity that is sufficient, the stomach can perfectly concoct and digest, and it sufficeth the due nourishment of the body.

A greater quantity of some things may be eaten than of others, some being of lighter digestion than others.

The difficulty lies, in finding out an exact measure; but eat for necessity, not pleasure, for lust knows not where necessity ends.

Wouldst thou enjoy a long life, a healthy body, and a vigorous mind, and be acquainted also with the wonderful works of God, labour in the first place to bring thy appetite into subjection to reason.

THE ART *of* PROCURING PLEASANT DREAMS

[1786]

AS a great part of our life is spent in sleep during which
we have sometimes pleasant and sometimes painful
dreams, it becomes of some consequence to obtain the
one kind and avoid the other; for whether real or imaginary,
pain is pain and pleasure is pleasure. If we can sleep without
dreaming, it is well that painful dreams are avoided. If while
we sleep we can have any pleasing dream, it is, as the French
say, *autant de gagné*, so much added to the pleasure of life.

To this end it is, in the first place, necessary to be careful in
preserving health, by due exercise and great temperance; for, in
sickness, the imagination is disturbed, and disagreeable, sometimes terrible, ideas are apt to present themselves. Exercise
should precede meals, not immediately follow them; the first
promotes, the latter, unless moderate, obstructs digestion. If,
after exercise, we feed sparingly, the digestion will be easy and
good, the body lightsome, the temper cheerful, and all the animal functions performed agreeably. Sleep, when it follows, will
be natural and undisturbed; while indolence, with full feeding,
occasions nightmares and horrors inexpressible; we fall from
precipices, are assaulted by wild beasts, murderers and demons,
and experience every variety of distress. Observe, however, that
the quantities of food and exercise are relative things; those

[35]

who move much may, and indeed ought to eat more; those who use little exercise should eat little. In general, mankind, since the improvement of cookery, eat about twice as much as nature requires. Suppers are not bad, if we have not dined; but restless nights naturally follow hearty suppers after full dinners. Indeed, as there is a difference in constitutions, some rest well after these meals; it costs them only a frightful dream and an apoplexy, after which they sleep till doomsday. Nothing is more common in the newspapers, than instances of people who, after eating a hearty supper, are found dead abed in the morning.

Another means of preserving health, to be attended to, is the having a constant supply of fresh air in your bed-chamber. It has been a great mistake, the sleeping in rooms exactly closed, and in beds surrounded by curtains. No outward air that may come in to you is so unwholesome as the unchanged air, often breathed, of a close chamber. As boiling water does not grow hotter by longer boiling, if the particles that receive greater heat can escape; so living bodies do not putrefy, if the particles, so fast as they become putrid, can be thrown off. Nature expels them by the pores of the skin and the lungs, and in a free, open air they are carried off; but in a close room we receive them again and again, though they become more and more corrupt. A number of persons crowded into a small room thus spoil the air in a few minutes, and even render it mortal as in the Black Hole at Calcutta. A single person is said to spoil only a gallon of air per minute, and therefore requires a longer time to spoil a chamber-full; but it is done, however, in proportion, and many putrid disorders hence have their origin. It is recorded of Methusalem, who, being the longest liver, may be supposed to have best preserved his health, that he slept always in the open air; for, when he had lived five hundred years, an angel said to him; "Arise, Methusalem, and build thee an house, for thou shalt live yet five hundred years longer." But Methusalem answered, and said, "If I am to live but five hundred years longer, it is not worth while to build me an house; I will sleep in the air, as I have been used to do." Physicians, after having for ages contended that the sick should not be indulged with fresh air, have at length discovered that it may do them good. It is therefore to be hoped, that they may in time discover likewise, that it is not hurtful to those who are in health, and that we may be then cured of the *aërophobia*, that at present distresses weak minds, and makes them choose to be stifled and poisoned, rather than leave open the window of a bed-chamber, or put down the glass of a coach.

Confined air, when saturated with perspirable matter, will not receive more; and that matter must remain in our bodies, and occasion diseases; but it gives some previous notice of its being about to be hurtful, by producing certain uneasiness, slight indeed at first, which as with regard to the lungs is a trifling sensation, and to the pores of the skin a kind of restlessness, which is difficult to describe, and few that feel it know the cause of it. But we may recollect, that sometimes on waking in the night, we have, if warmly covered, found it difficult to get asleep again. We turn often without finding repose in any position. This fidgettiness (to use a vulgar expression for want of a better) is occasioned wholly by an uneasiness in the skin, owing to the retention of the perspirable matter—the bed-clothes having received their quantity, and, being saturated, refusing to take any more. To become sensible of this by an experiment, let a person keep his position in the bed, but throw off the bed-clothes, and suffer fresh air to approach the part uncovered of his body; he will then feel that part suddenly refreshed; for the air will immediately relieve the skin, by receiving, licking up, and carrying off, the load of perspirable matter that incommoded it. For every portion of cool air that approaches the warm skin, in receiving its part of that vapour, receives therewith a degree of heat that rarefies and renders it lighter, when it will be pushed away with its burthen, by cooler and therefore heavier fresh air, which for a moment supplies its place, and then, being likewise changed and warmed, gives way to a succeeding quantity. This is the order of nature, to prevent animals being infected by their own perspiration. He will now be sensible of the difference between the part exposed to the air and that which, remaining sunk in the bed, denies the air access: for this part now manifests its uneasiness more distinctly by the comparison, and the seat of the uneasiness is more plainly perceived than when the whole surface of the body was affected by it.

Here, then, is one great and general cause of unpleasing dreams. For when the body is uneasy, the mind will be disturbed by it, and disagreeable ideas of various kinds will in sleep be the natural consequences. The remedies, preventive and curative, follow:

1. By eating moderately (as before advised for health's sake) less perspirable matter is produced in a given time; hence the bed-clothes receive it longer before they are saturated, and we may therefore sleep longer before we are made uneasy by their refusing to receive any more.

2. By using thinner and more porous bed-clothes, which will

suffer the perspirable matter more easily to pass through them, we are less incommoded, such being longer tolerable.

3. When you are awakened by this uneasiness, and find you cannot easily sleep again, get out of bed, beat up and turn your pillow, shake the bed-clothes well, with at least twenty shakes, then throw the bed open and leave it to cool; in the meanwhile, continuing undrest, walk about your chamber till your skin has had time to discharge its load, which it will do sooner as the air may be dried and colder. When you begin to feel the cold air unpleasant, then return to your bed, and you will soon fall asleep, and your sleep will be sweet and pleasant. All the scenes presented to your fancy will be too of the pleasing kind. I am often as agreeably entertained with them, as by the scenery of an opera. If you happen to be too indolent to get out of bed, you may, instead of it, lift up your bed-clothes with one arm and leg, so as to draw in a good deal of fresh air, and by letting them fall force it out again. This, repeated twenty times, will so clear them of the perspirable matter they have imbibed, as to permit your sleeping well for some time afterwards. But this latter method is not equal to the former.

Those who do not love trouble, and can afford to have two beds, will find great luxury in rising, when they wake in a hot bed, and going into the cool one. Such shifting of beds would also be of great service to persons ill of a fever, as it refreshes and frequently procures sleep. A very large bed, that will admit a removal so distant from the first situation as to be cool and sweet, may in a degree answer the same end.

One or two observations more will conclude this little piece. Care must be taken, when you lie down, to dispose your pillow so as to suit your manner of placing your head, and to be perfectly easy; then place your limbs so as not to bear inconveniently hard upon one another, as for instance, the joints of your ankles; for, though a bad position may at first give but little pain and be hardly noticed, yet a continuance will render it less tolerable, and the uneasiness may come on while you are asleep, and disturb your imagination. These are the rules of the art. But, though they will generally prove effectual in producing the end intended, there is a case in which the most punctual observance of them will be totally fruitless. I need not mention the case to you, my dear friend, but my account of the art would be imperfect without it. The case is, when the person who desires to have pleasant dreams has not taken care to preserve, what is necessary above all things,

A GOOD CONSCIENCE..

LEARNING TO SWIM

TO

OLIVER NEAVE

DEAR SIR,

I CANNOT be of opinion with you that it is too late in life for you to learn to swim. The river near the bottom of your garden affords a most convenient place for the purpose. And as your new employment requires your being often on the water, of which you have such a dread, I think you would do well to make the trial; nothing being so likely to remove those apprehensions as the consciousness of an ability to swim to the shore, in case of an accident, or of supporting yourself in the water till a boat could come to take you up. I do not know how far corks or bladders may be useful in learning to swim, having never seen much trial of them. Possibly they may be of service in supporting the body while you are learning what is called the stroke, or that manner of drawing in and striking out the hands and feet that is necessary to produce progressive motion. But you will be no swimmer till you can place some confidence in the power of the water to support you; I would therefore advise the acquiring that confidence in the first place; especially as I have known several, who, by a little of the practice necessary for that purpose, have insensibly acquired the stroke, taught as it were by nature.

The practice I mean is this. Choosing a place where the water deepens gradually, walk cooly into it till it is up to your breast, then turn round, your face to the shore, and throw an egg into the water between you and the shore. It will sink to the bottom, and be easily seen there, as your water is clear. It must lie in water so deep as that you cannot reach it to take it up but by diving for it. To encourage yourself in order to do this, reflect that your progress will be from deeper to shallower water, and that at any time you may, by bringing your legs under you and standing on the bottom, raise your head far above the water. Then plunge under it with your eyes open, throwing yourself towards the egg, and endeavouring by the action of your hands and feet against the water to get forward till within reach of it. In this attempt you will find, that the water buoys you up against your inclination; that it is not so easy a thing to sink as you imagined; that you cannot but by active force get down to the egg. Thus you feel the power of the water to support you, and learn to confide in that power; while your endeavours to overcome it, and to reach the egg, teach you the manner of acting on the water with your feet and hands, which action is afterwards used in swimming to support your head higher above water, or to go forward through it.

I would the more earnestly press you to the trial of this method, because, though I think I satisfied you that your body is lighter than water, and that you might float in it a long time with your mouth free for breathing, if you would put yourself in a proper posture, and would be still and forbear struggling; yet till you have obtained this experimental confidence in the water, I cannot depend on your having the necessary presence of mind to recollect that posture and the directions I gave you relating to it. The surprise may put all out of your mind. For though we value ourselves on being reasonable, knowing creatures, reason and knowledge seem on such occasions to be of little use to us; and the brutes, to whom we allow scarce a glimmering of either, appear to have the advantage of us.

I will, however, take this opportunity of repeating those particulars to you which I mentioned in our last conversation, as, by perusing them at your leisure, you may possibly imprint them so in your memory as on occasion to be of some use to you.

1. That though the legs, arms, and head, of a human body, being solid parts, are specifically something heavier than fresh water, yet the trunk, particularly the upper part, from its hollowness, is so much lighter than water, as that the whole of the body taken together is too light to sink wholly under water, but some part will remain above, until the lungs become filled with water, which happens from drawing water into them instead of air, when a person in the fright attempts breathing while the mouth and nostrils are under water.

2. That the legs and arms are specifically lighter than salt water, and will be supported by it, so that a human body would not sink in salt water, though the lungs were filled as above, but from the greater specific gravity of the head.

3. That therefore a person throwing himself on his back in salt water, and extending his arms, may easily lie so as to keep his mouth and nostrils free for breathing; and by a small motion of his hands may prevent turning, if he should perceive any tendency to it.

4. That in fresh water, if a man throws himself on his back, near the surface, he cannot long continue in that situation but by proper action of his hands on the water. If he uses no such action, the legs and lower part of the body will gradually sink till

he comes into an upright position, in which he will continue suspended, the hollow of the breast keeping the head uppermost.

5. But if, in this erect position, the head is kept upright above the shoulders, as when we stand on the ground, the immersion will, by the weight of that part of the head that is out of water, reach above the mouth and nostrils, perhaps a little above the eyes, so that a man cannot long remain suspended in water with his head in that position.

6. The body continuing suspended as before, and upright, if the head be leaned quite back, so that the face looks upwards, all the back part of the head being then under water, and its weight consequently in a great measure supported by it, the face will remain above water quite free for breathing, will rise an inch higher every inspiration, and sink as much every expiration, but never so low as that the water may come over the mouth.

7. If therefore a person, unacquainted with swimming and falling accidentally into the water, could have presence of mind sufficient to avoid struggling and plunging, and let the body take this natural position, he might continue long safe from drowning till perhaps help would come. For as to the clothes, their additional weight while immersed is very inconsiderable, the water supporting it, though when he comes out of the water, he would find them very heavy indeed.

But, as I said before, I would not advise you or any one to depend on having this presence of mind on such an occasion, but learn fairly to swim; as I wish all men were taught to do in their youth. They would, on many occurrences, be the safer for having that skill, and on many more the happier, as freer from painful apprehensions of danger, to say nothing of the enjoyment in so delightful and wholesome an exercise. Soldiers particularly should, methinks, all be taught to swim; it might be of frequent use either in surprising an enemy, or saving themselves. And if I had now boys to educate, I should prefer those schools (other things being equal) where an opportunity was afforded for acquiring so advantageous an art, which, once learned, is never forgotten.

I am, Sir, &c.

B. FRANKLIN.

ON SWIMMING

I AM apprehensive, that I shall not be able to find leisure for making all the disquisitions and experiments which would be desirable on this subject. I must, therefore, content myself with a few remarks.

The specific gravity of some human bodies, in comparison to that of water, has been examined by Mr. Robinson, in our Philosophical Transactions, Volume L., page 30, for the year 1757. He asserts, that fat persons with small bones float most easily upon the water.

The diving-bell is accurately described in our Transactions.

When I was a boy, I made two oval palettes, each about ten inches long, and six broad, with a hole for the thumb, in order to retain it fast in the palm of my hand. They much resembled a painter's palletes. In swimming I pushed the edges of these forward, and I struck the water with their flat surfaces as I drew them back. I remember I swam faster by means of these pallets, but they fatigued my wrists. I also fitted to the soles of my feet a kind of sandals; but I was not satisfied with them, because I observed that the stroke is partly given by the inside of the feet and the ancles, and not entirely with the soles of the feet.

* This letter is in reply to Dubourg's letter dated February 12, 1773.

We have here waistcoats for swimming, which are made of double sailcloth, with small pieces of cork quilted in between them.

I know nothing of the *scaphandre* of M. de la Chapelle.

I know by experience, that it is a great comfort to a swimmer, who has a considerable distance to go, to turn himself sometimes on his back, and to vary in other respects the means of procuring a progressive motion.

When he is seized with the cramp in the leg, the method of driving it away is, to give to the parts affected a sudden, vigorous, and violent shock; which he may do in the air as he swims on his back.

During the great heats of summer there is no danger in bathing, however warm we may be, in rivers which have been thoroughly warmed by the sun. But to throw one's self into cold spring water, when the body has been heated by exercise in the sun, is an imprudence which may prove fatal. I once knew an instance of four young men, who, having worked at harvest in the heat of the day, with a view of refreshing themselves plunged into a spring of cold water; two died upon the spot, a third the next morning, and the fourth recovered with great difficulty. A copious draught of cold water, in similar circumstances, is frequently attended with the same effect in North America.

The exercise of swimming is one of the most healthy and agreeable in the world. After having swam for an hour or two in the evening, one sleeps cooly the whole night, even during the most ardent heat of summer. Perhaps, the pores being cleansed, the insensible perspiration increases and occasions this coolness. It is certain that much swimming is the means of stopping a diarrhœa, and even of producing a constipation. With respect to those, who do not know how to swim, or who are affected with a diarrhœa at a season which does not permit them to use that exercise, a warm bath, by cleansing and purifying the skin, is found very salutary, and often effects a radical cure. I speak from my own experience, frequently repeated, and that of others, to whom I have recommended this.

You will not be displeased if I conclude these hasty remarks by informing you, that as the ordinary method of swimming is reduced to the act of rowing with the arms and legs, and is consequently a laborious and fatiguing operation when the space of water to be crossed is considerable; there is a method in which a swimmer may pass to great distances with much facility, by means of a sail. This discovery I fortunately made by accident, and in the following manner.

When I was a boy, I amused myself one day with flying a paper kite; and approaching the bank of a pond, which was near a mile broad, I tied the string to a stake, and the kite ascended to a very considerable height above the pond, while I was swimming. In a little time, being desirous of amusing myself with my kite, and enjoying at the same time the pleasure of swimming, I returned; and, loosing from the stake the string with the little stick which was fastened to it, went again into the water, where I found, that, lying on my back and holding the stick in my hands, I was drawn along the surface of the water in a very agreeable manner. Having then engaged another boy to carry my clothes round the pond, to a place which I pointed out to him on the other side, I began to cross the pond with my kite, which carried me quite over without the least fatigue, and with the greatest pleasure imaginable. I was only obliged occasionally to halt a little in my course, and resist its progress, when it appeared that, by following too quick, I lowered the kite too much; by doing which occasionally I made it rise again. I have never since that time practised this singular mode of swimming, though I think it not impossible to cross in this manner from Dover to Calais. The packet-boat, however, is still preferable.

B. FRANKLIN.

CHOOSING EYE-GLASSES

TO

MRS. JANE MECOM

London, July 17, 1771

DEAR SISTER,

I HAVE received your kind letter of May 10. You seem so sensible of your error in so hastily suspecting me, that I am now in my turn sorry I took notice of it. Let us then suppose that accompt ballanced and settled, and think no more of it.—

In some former letter I believe I mention'd the price of the books, which I have now forgotten: But I think it was 3 S each. — To be sure there are objections to the Doctrine of Pre-existence. But it seems to have been invented with a good intention, to save the honour of the Diety, which was thought to be injured by the supposition of his bringing creatures into the world to be miserable, without any previous misbehavior of theirs to deserve it. This, however, is perhaps an officious supporting of the Ark, without being call'd to such service. Where he has thought fit to draw a veil, our attempting to remove it may be deem'd at least an offensive impertinence, and we shall probably succeed little better in such an adventure to gain forbidden knowledge, than our first parents did when they ate the apples. —

I meant no more by saying mankind were devils to one another, than that being in general superior to the malice of the other creatures, they were not so much tormented by them as by themselves. — Upon the whole I am much disposed to like the world as I find it, & to doubt my own judgement as to what would mend it. I see so much wisdom in what I understand of its creations and government, that I suspect equal wisdom may be in what I do not understand. And thence have perhaps as much trust in God as the most pious Christian. —

I am very happy that a good understanding continues between you and the Philadelphia folks. Our father, who was a very wise man us'd to say, nothing was more common than for those who lov'd one another at a distance, to find many causes of dislike when they came together; and therefore he did not approve of visits to relations in distant places, which could not well be short enough for them to part good friends. — I saw a proof of it, in the disgusts between him and his brother Benjamin; and tho' I was a child I still remember how affectionate their correspondence was while they were separated, and the disputes and misunderstandings they had when they came to live some time together in the same house. — But you have been more prudent, and restrain'd that "aptness" you say you have "to interfere in other people's oeconomical affairs by putting in a word now and then unasked." And so all's well that ends well.—

I thought you had mentioned in one of your letters a desire to have spectacles of some sort sent you; but I cannot now find such a letter. However I send you a pair of every size of glasses from 1 to 13. To suit yourself, take out a pair at a time, and hold one of the glasses first against one eye, and then against the other, looking on some small print. — If the first suits neither eye, put them up again before you open a second. Thus you will keep them from mixing. By trying and comparing at your leisure, you may find those that are best for you, which you cannot well do in a shop, where for want of time and care, people often take such as strain their eyes and hurt them. I advise your trying each of your eyes separately, because few peoples eyes are fellows, and almost every body in reading or working uses one eye principally, the other being dimmer or perhaps fitter for distant objects; and thence it happens that the spectacles whose glasses are fellows suit sometimes that eye which before was not used tho' they do not suit the other. — When you have suited your self, keep the higher numbers for future use as your eyes may grow older; and oblige your friends with the others.

I was lately at Sheffield and Birmingham, where I bought a few plated things which I send you as tokens, viz. A pair of sauceboats, a pair of flat candlesticks, and a saucepan, lined with silver. Please to accept of them. I have had one of the latter in constant use 12 years, and the silver still holds. But tinning is soon gone.

Mʳˢ Stevenson and Mʳˢ Hewson present their compliments. The latter has a fine son. Sally Franklin sends her duty to you. I wonder you have not heard of her till lately. She has liv'd with me these 5 years, a very good girl, now near 16. She is great grandaughter of our father's brother John, who was a dyer at Banbury in Oxfordshire, where our grandfather Thomas lies buried. I saw his gravestone. Sally's father, John's grandson, is now living at Lutterworth in Leicestershire, where he follows the same business, his father too being bred a dyer, as was our uncle Benjamin. He is a widower, & Sally his only child. These two are the only descendants of our grandfather Thomas now remaining in England that retain the name of *Franklin*. The Walkers are descended of John by a daughter that I have seen, lately deceased. Sally and cousin William's children, & Henry Walker who now attends Josiah are relations in the same degree to one another and to your & my grandchildren, viz.

[Here Franklin had drawn a genealogical map]
What is this relation called? Is it third cousins? — Having mentioned so many dyers in our family, I will now it's in my mind to request of you a full & particular receipt for dying worsted of that beautiful red, which you learnt of our mother.— And also a receipt for making crown soap. Let it be very exact in the smallest particulars. Enclos'd I send you a receipt for making soft soap in the sun.—

I have never seen any young men from America that acquir'd by their behavior here more general esteem than those you recommended to me. Josiah has stuck close to his musical studies and still continues them. Jonathan has been diligent in business for his friends as well as himself, obliging to everybody, tender of his brother, not fond of the expensive amusements of the place, regular in his hours, and spending what leisure hours he had in the study of mathematics. He goes home to settle in business and I think there is great probability of his doing well.

With best wishes for you & all yours, I am ever,

Your affectionate brother,
B. FRANKLIN.

I have mislaid the soap receipt
but will send it when I find it.

BIFOCALS

TO

GEORGE WHATLEY

Passy, May 23, 1785.

B Y Mr. Dollond's saying, that my double spectacles can only serve particular eyes, I doubt he has not been rightly informed of their construction. I imagine it will be found pretty generally true, that the same convexity of glass, through which a man sees clearest and best at the distance proper for reading, is not the best for greater distances. I therefore had formerly two pair of spectacles, which I shifted occasionally, as in travelling I sometimes read, and often wanted to regard the prospects. Finding this change troublesome, and not always sufficiently ready, I had the glasses cut, and half of each kind associated in the same circle, thus,

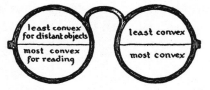

By this means, as I wear my spectacles constantly, I have only to move my eyes up or down, as I want to see distinctly far or

near, the proper glasses being always ready. This I find more particularly convenient since my being in France, the glasses that serve me best at table to see what I eat, not being the best to see the faces of those on the other side of the table who speak to me; and when one's ears are not well accustomed to the sounds of a language, a sight of the movements in the features of him that speaks helps to explain; so that I understand French better by the help of my spectacles.

.   .   .   .

B. FRANKLIN.

OF LIGHTNING *and the* METHOD *(now used in America) of* SECURING BUILDINGS *and* PERSONS
from its mischievous effects

Paris, Sept., 1767.

EXPERIMENTS made in electricity first gave philosophers a suspicion that the matter of lightning was the same with the electric matter. Experiments afterwards made on lightning obtained from the clouds by pointed rods, received into bottles, and subjected to every trial, have since proved this suspicion to be perfectly well founded; and that whatever properties we find in electricity, are also the properties of lightning.

This matter of lightning, or of electricity, is an extream subtile fluid, penetrating other bodies, and subsisting in them, equally diffused.

When by any operation of art or nature, there happens to be a greater proportion of this fluid in one body than in another, the body which has most will communicate to that which has least, till the proportion becomes equal; provided the distance between them be not too great; or, if it is too great, till there be proper conductors to convey it from one to the other.

If the communication be through the air without any conductor, a bright light is seen between the bodies, and a sound is heard. In our small experiments we call this light and sound the electric spark and snap; but in the great operations of nature, the light is what we call *lightning,* and the sound (produced at the same time, tho' generally arriving later at our ears than the light does to our eyes) is, with its echoes, called *thunder.*

If the communication of this fluid is by a conductor, it may be without either light or sound, the subtle fluid passing in the substance of the conductor.

If the conductor be good and of sufficient bigness, the fluid passes through it without hurting it. If otherwise, it is damaged or destroyed.

All metals, and water, are good conductors. Other bodies may become conductors by having some quantity of water in them, as wood, and other materials used in building, but not having much water in them, they are not good conductors, and therefore are often damaged in the operation.

Glass, wax, silk, wool, hair, feathers, and even wood, perfectly dry are nonconductors: that is, they resist instead of facilitating the passage of this suble [sic] fluid.

When this fluid has an opportunity of passing through two conductors, one good, and sufficient, as of metal, the other not so good, it passes in the best, and will follow it in any direction.

The distance at which a body charged with this fluid will discharge itself suddenly, striking through the air into another body that is not charged, or not so highly charg'd, is different according to the quantity of the fluid, the dimensions and form of the bodies themselves, and the state of the air between them. This distance, whatever it happens to be between any two bodies, is called their *striking distance,* as till they come within that distance of each other, no stroke will be made.

The clouds have often more of this fluid in proportion than the earth; in which case as soon as they come near enough (that is, within the striking distance) or meet with a conductor, the fluid quits them and strikes into the earth. A cloud fully charged with this fluid, if so high as to be beyond the striking distance from the earth, passes quietly without making noise or giving light; unless it meets with other clouds that have less.

Tall trees, and lofty buildings, as the towers and spires of churches, become sometimes conductors between the clouds and the earth; but not being good ones, that is, not conveying the fluid freely, they are often damaged.

Buildings that have their roofs covered with lead, or other metal, and spouts of metal continued from the roof into the ground to carry off the water, are never hurt by lightning, as, whenever it falls on such a building, it passes in the metals and not in the walls.

When other buildings happen to be within the striking distance from such clouds, the fluid passes in the walls whether of wood, brick or stone, quitting the walls only when it can find better conductors near them, as metal rods, bolts, and hinges of windows or doors, gilding on wainscot, or frames of pictures; the silvering on the backs of looking-glasses; the wires for bells; and the bodies of animals, as containing watry fluids. And in passing thro' the house it follows the direction of these conductors, taking as many in it's way as can assist it in its passage, whether in a strait or crooked line, leaping from one to the other, if not far distant from each other, only rending the wall in the spaces where these partial good conductors are too distant from each other.

An iron rod being placed on the outside of a building, from

the highest part continued down into the moist earth, in any direction, strait or crooked, following the form of the roof or other parts of the building, will receive the lightning at its upper end, attracting it so as to prevent its striking any other part; and, affording it a good conveyance into the earth, will prevent its damaging any part of the building.

A small quantity of metal is found able to conduct a great quantity of this fluid. A wire no bigger than a goose'quill, has been known to conduct (with safety to the building as far as the wire was continued) a quantity of lightning that did prodigious damage both above and below it; and probably larger rods are not necessary, tho' it is common in America, to make them of half an inch, some of three quarters, or an inch diameter.

The rod may be fastened to the wall, chimney, &c. with staples of iron. The lightning will not leave the rod (a good conductor) to pass into the wall (a bad conductor), through those staples. It would rather, if any were in the wall, pass out of it into the rod to get more readily by that conductor into the earth.

If the building be very large and extensive, two or more rods may be placed at different parts, for greater security.

Small ragged parts of clouds suspended in the air between the great body of clouds and the earth (like leaf gold in electrical experiments), often serve as partial conductors for the lightning, which proceeds from one of them to another, and by their help comes within the striking distance to the earth or a building. It therefore strikes through those conductors a building that would otherwise be out of the striking distance.

Long sharp points communicating with the earth, and presented to such parts of clouds, drawing silently from them the fluid they are charged with, they are then attracted to the cloud, and may leave the distance so great as to be beyond the reach of striking.

It is therefore that we elevate the upper end of the rod six or eight feet above the highest part of the building, tapering it gradually to a fine sharp point, which is gilt to prevent its rusting.

Thus the pointed rod either prevents a stroke from the cloud, or, if a stroke is made, conducts it to the earth with safety to the building.

The lower end of the rod should enter the earth so deep as to come at the moist part, perhaps two or three feet; and, if bent when under the surface so as to go in a horizontal line six or eight feet from the wall, and then bent again downwards three or four feet, it will prevent damage to any of the stones of the foundation.

A person apprehensive of danger from lightning, happening during the time of thunder to be in a house not so secured, will do well to avoid sitting near the chimney, near a looking-glass, or any gilt pictures or wainscot; the safest place is in the middle of the room, (so it be not under a metal lustre suspended by a chain) sitting in one chair and laying the feet up in another. It is still safer to bring two or three mattrasses or beds into the middle of the room, and folding them up double, place the chair upon them; for they not being so good conductors as the walls, the lightning will not chuse an interrupted course through the air of the room and the bedding, when it can go thro' a continued better conductor the wall. But, where it can be had, a hamock or swinging bed, suspended by silk cords equally distant from the walls on every side, and from the cieling and floor above and below, affords the safest situation a person can have in any room whatever; and what indeed may be deemed quite free from danger of any stroke by lightning.

B. F.

ADVANTAGE OF POINTED
CONDUCTORS

[1772 ?]

SIR

· · · · · · · · · · · ·

POINTED conductors to secure buildings from lightning
have now been in use near 20 years in America, and
are there become so common, that numbers of them appear on private houses in every street of the principal towns, besides those on churches, public buildings, magazines of powder,
and gentlemen's seats in the country. Thunder storms are much
more frequent there than in Europe, and hitherto there has
been no instance of a house so guarded being damaged by lightning; for wherever it has broke over any of them the point has
always received it, & the conductor has convey'd it safely into
the earth, of which we have now 5 authentick instances. Here in
England, the practice has made a slower progress, damage by
lightning being less frequent, & people of course less apprehensive of danger from it; yet besides St. Paul's Church, St.
James's Church, the Queen's Palace & Blenheim House a number of private Gentlemen's seats round the town are now provided with conductors, and the ships bound to the east & W
Indies & the Coast of Guinea begin to supply themselves with
chains for that purpose made by Mr. Nairne, especially since
the return of Messrs Banks & Solander, who relate that their

ship was as they think saved by one of those chains from damage when a Dutch man of war lying near them in the Road of Batavia was almost demolished by the lightning.

.　　.　　.　　.　　.　　.　　.　　.　　.　　.　　.

Sir

Your most obedient

humble servant

B. FRANKLIN.

PENNSYLVANIAN FIREPLACES

Wherein

Their construction and manner of operation is particularly explained; their advantages above every other method of warming rooms demonstrated; and all objections that have been raised against the use of them answered and obviated. With directions for putting them up, and for using them to the best advantage. And a copper-plate in which the several parts of the machine are exactly laid down, from a scale of equal parts.

1744

IN these northern colonies the inhabitants keep fires to sit by, generally *seven months* in the year; that is, from the beginning of *October* to the end of *April;* and in some winters near *eight months,* by taking in part of *September* and *May.*

Wood, our common fewel, which within these 100 years might be had at every man's door, must now be fetch'd near 100 miles to some towns, and makes a very considerable article in the expence of families.

As therefore so much of the comfort and conveniency of our lives, for so great a part of the year, depends on the article of *fire;* since Fuel is become so expensive, and (as the country is more clear'd and settled) will of course grow scarcer and dearer; any new proposal for saving the wood, and for lessening the charge and augmenting the benefit of fire, by some particular method of making and managing it, may at least be thought worth consideration.

The New Fire-Places are a late invention to that purpose, (experienced now three winters, by a great number of families in *Pennsylvania*) of which this paper is intended to give a particular account.

That the reader may the better judge whether this method of managing fire has any advantage over those heretofore in use, it may be proper to consider both the old and new methods, separately and particularly, and afterwards make the comparison.

In order to this 'tis necessary to understand well some few of the properties of air and fire, *viz.*

1. Air is rarified by *heat*, and condens'd by *cold*, *i.e.* the same quantity of air takes up more space when warm than when cold. This may be shown by several very easy experiments. Take any clear glass bottle (a *Florence* flask stript of the straw is best), place it before the fire, and, as the air within is warm'd and rarified, part of it will be driven out of the bottle; turn it up, place its mouth in a vessel of water, and remove it from the fire; then, as the air within cools and contracts, you will see the water rise in the neck of the bottle, supplying the place of just so much air as was driven out. Hold a large hot coal near the side of the bottle, and as the air within feels the heat, it will again distend and force out the water. Or, fill a bladder half-full of air, tie the neck tight, and lay it before a fire as near as may be without scorching the bladder; as the air within heats, you will perceive it to swell and fill the bladder, till it becomes tight, as if full blown: Remove it to a cool place, and you will see it fall gradually, till it becomes as lank as at first.

2. Air rarified and distended by heat is specifically lighter than it was before, and will rise in other air of greater density.

As wood, oil, or any other matter specifically lighter than water, if plac'd at the bottom of a vessel of water, will rise till it comes to the top; so rarified air will rise in common air, till it either comes to air of equal weight, or is by cold reduc'd to its former density.

A fire then being made in any chimney, the air over the fire is rarified by the heat, becomes lighter and therefore immediately rises in the funnel, and goes out; the other air in the room (flowing towards the chimney) supplies its place, is rarified in its turn, and rises likewise; the place of the air thus carried out of the room is supplied by fresh air coming in thro' doors and windows, or, if they be shut, thro' every crevice with violence, as may be seen by holding a candle to a key-hole: If the room be so tight as that all the crevices together will not supply so much air as is continually carried off, then in a little time the current up the funnel must flag, and the smoke, being no longer driven up must come into the room.

1. Fire (*i.e.* common fire) throws out light, heat, and smoke (or fume). The two first move in right lines, and with great swiftness; the latter is but just separated from the fuel, and then moves only as it is carried by the stream of rarified air. And without a continual accession and recession of air, to carry off the smoaky fumes, they would remain crouded about the fire, and stifle it.

2. Heat may be separated from the smoke as well as from the light, by means of a plate of iron, which will suffer heat to pass through it without the others.

3. Fire sends out its rays of heat, as well as rays of light, equally every way: But the greatest sensible heat is over the fire, where there is, besides the rays of heat shot upwards, a con-

tinual rising stream of hot air, heated by the rays shot round on every side. . . .

[The account now proceeds to discuss the fireplaces hitherto in use, and to describe the new fireplace in detail, giving instructions for using it. Ed.]

The Advantages of this Fire-place

Its advantages above the common fire-places are,

1. That your whole room is equally warmed; so that people need not croud so close round the fire, but may sit near the window, and have the benefit of the light for reading, writing, needlework, &c. They may sit with comfort in any part of the room, which is a very considerable advantage in a large family, where there must often be two fires kept, because all cannot conveniently come at one.

2. If you sit near the fire, you have not that cold draught of uncomfortable air nipping your back and heels, as when before common fires, by which many catch cold, being scorcht before, and, as it were, froze behind.

3. If you sit against a crevice, there is not that sharp draught of cold air playing on you, as in rooms where there are fires in the common way; by which many catch cold, whence proceed coughs, catarrhs, tooth-achs, fevers, pleurisies, and many other diseases.

4. In case of sickness, they make most excellent nursing-rooms; as they constantly supply a sufficiency of fresh air, so warmed at the same time as to be no way inconvenient or dangerous. A small one does well in a chamber; and, the chimneys being fitted for it, it may be remov'd from one room to another, as occasion requires, and fix'd in half an hour. The equal tem-

per, too, and warmth, of the air of the room, is thought to be particularly advantageous in some distempers: For 'twas observ'd in the winters of 1730 and 1736, when the small-pox spread in *Pennsylvania,* that very few of the children of the *Germans* died of that distemper in proportion to those of the *English;* which was ascrib'd by some to the warmth and equal temper of air in their stove-rooms; which made the disease as favourable as it commonly is in the *West Indies.* But this conjecture we submit to the judgment of physicians.

5. In common chimneys, the strongest heat from the fire, which is upwards, goes directly up the chimney, and is lost; and there is such a strong draught into the chimney, that not only the upright heat, but also back, sides, and downward heats, are carried up the chimney by that draught of air; and the warmth given before the fire, by the rays that strike out towards the room, is continually driven back, crouded into the chimney, and carried up, by the same draught of air. But here the upright heat strikes and heats the top plate, which warms the air above it, and that comes into the room. The heat likewise, which the fire communicates to the sides, back bottom, and air-box, is all brought into the room; for you will find a constant current of warm air coming out of the chimney-corner into the room. Hold a candle just under the mantle-piece, or breast of your chimney, and you will see the flame bent outwards: By laying a piece of smoaking paper on the hearth, on either side, you may see how the current of air moves, and where it tends, for it will turn and carry the smoke with it.

6. Thus, as very little of the heat is lost, when this fire-place is us'd, *much less wood* will serve you, which is a considerable advantage where wood is dear.

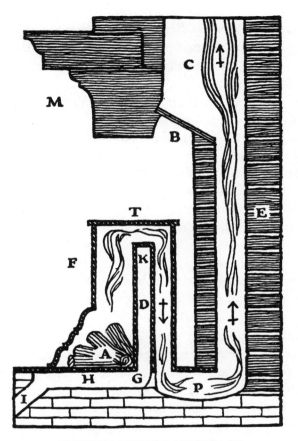

PENNSYLVANIAN FIREPLACE

M. The Mantle-piece or Breast of the Chimney. *C*. The Funnel. *B*. The false Back and Closing. *E*. True Back of the Chimney. *T*. Top of the Fireplace. *F*. The Front of it. *A*. The Place where the Fire is made. *D*. The Air-Box. *K*. The Hole in the Side-plate, thro' which the warm'd Air is discharged out of the Air-Box into the Room. *H*. The Hollow fill'd with fresh Air, entring at the Passage *I*, and ascending into the Air-Box thro' the Air-hole in the Bottom-plate near *G*. The Partition in the Hollow to keep the Air and Smoke apart. *P*. The Passage under the False Back and Part of the Hearth for the Smoke. ↑ The Course of the Smoke.

7. When you burn candles near this fire-place, you will find that the flame burns quite upright, and does not blare and run the tallow down, by drawing towards the chimney, as against common fires.

8. This fire-place cures most smoaky chimneys, and thereby preserves both the eyes and furniture.

9. It prevents the fouling of chimneys; much of the lint and dust that contributes to foul a chimney, being by the low arch oblig'd to pass thro' the flame, where 'tis consum'd. Then less wood being burnt, there is less smoke made. Again, the shutter, or trap-bellows, soon blowing the wood into a flame, the same wood does not yield so much smoke as if burnt in a common chimney: For as soon as flame begins, smoke, in proportion, ceases.

10. And, if a chimney should be foul, 'tis much less likely to take fire. If it should take fire, 'tis easily stifled and extinguished.

11. A fire may be very speedily made in this fire-place, by the help of the shutter, or trap-bellows, as aforesaid.

12. A fire may be soon extinguished by closing it with the shutter before, and turning the register behind, which will stifle it, and the brands will remain ready to rekindle.

13. The room being once warm, the warmth may be retain'd in it all night.

14. And lastly, the fire is so secur'd at night, that not one spark can fly out into the room to do damage.

With all these conveniencies, you do not lose the pleasing sight nor use of the fire, as in the Dutch stoves, but may boil the tea-kettle, warm the flat-irons, heat heaters, keep warm a dish of victuals by setting it on the top, &c. &c.

SLAUGHTERING *by* ELECTRICITY

TO

Barbeu Dubourg *and* Thomas François Dalibard

[1773]

MY DEAR FRIENDS,

MY answer to your questions concerning the mode of rendering meat tender by electricity, can only be founded upon conjecture; for I have not experiments enough to warrant the facts. All that I can say at present is, that I think electricity might be employed for this purpose, and I shall state what follows as the observations or reasons which make me presume so.

It has been observed that lightning, by rarefying and reducing into vapour the moisture contained in solid wood, in an oak, for instance, has forcibly separated its fibres, and broken it into small splinters; that, by penetrating intimately the hardest metals, as iron, it has separated the parts in an instant, so as to convert a perfect solid into a state of fluidity; it is not then improbable, that the same subtile matter, passing through the bodies of animals with rapidity, should possess sufficient force to produce an effect nearly similar.

The flesh of animals, fresh killed in the usual manner, is firm, hard, and not in a very eatable state, because the particles adhere too forcibly to each other. At a certain period, the cohesion is weakened, and, in its progress towards putrefaction, which tends to produce a total separation, the flesh becomes what we call tender, or is in that state most proper to be used as our food.

It has frequently been remarked, that animals killed by lightning putrefy immediately. This cannot be invariably the case, since a quantity of lightning, sufficient to kill, may not be sufficient to tear and divide the fibres and particles of flesh, and reduce them to that tender state, which is the prelude to putrefaction. Hence it is, that some animals killed in this manner will keep longer than others. But the putrefaction sometimes proceeds with surprising celerity. A respectable person assured me that he once knew a remarkable instance of this. A whole flock of sheep in Scotland, being closely assembled under a tree, were killed by a flash of lightning; and, it being rather late in the evening, the proprietor, desirous of saving something, sent persons early the next morning to flay them; but the putrefaction was such, and the stench so abominable, that they had not the courage to execute their orders, and the bodies were accordingly buried in their skins. It is not unreasonable to presume, that, between the period of their death and that of their putrefaction, a time intervened in which the flesh might be only tender, and only sufficiently so to be served at table. Add to this, that persons, who have eaten of fowls killed by our feeble imitation of lightning, (electricity), and dressed immediately, have asserted, that the flesh was remarkably tender.

The little utility of this practice has perhaps prevented its being much adopted. For, though it sometimes happens, that a company unexpectedly arriving at a country-house, or an unusual conflux of travellers to an inn, may render it necessary to kill a number of animals for immediate use; yet, as travellers have commonly a good appetite, little attention has been paid to the trifling inconvenience of having their meat a little tough. As this kind of death is nevertheless, more sudden, and consequently less severe, than any other, if this should operate as a motive with compassionate persons to employ it for animals sacrificed for their use, they may conduct the process thus.

Having prepared a battery of six large glass jars (each from twenty to twenty-four pints) as for the Leyden experiment, and having established a communication, as usual, from the interior surface of each with the prime conductor, and having given them a full charge (which, with a good machine, may be executed in a few minutes, and may be estimated by an electrometer), a chain which communicates with the exterior of the jars must be wrapped round the thighs of the fowl; after which the operator, holding it by the wings, turned back and made to touch behind, must raise it so high that the head may receive the first shock from the prime conductor. The animal dies instantly. Let the head be immediately cut off to make it bleed, when it may be plucked and dressed immediately. This quantity of electricity is supposed sufficient for a turkey of ten pounds weight, and perhaps for a lamb. Experience alone will inform us of the requisite proportions for animals of different forms and ages. Probably not less will be required to render a small bird, which is very old, tender, than for a larger one, which is young. It is easy to furnish the requisite quantity of electricity, by employing a greater or less number of jars. As six jars, however, discharged at once, are capable of giving a very violent shock, the operator must be very circumspect, lest he should happen to make the experiment on his own flesh, instead of that of the fowl.

B. FRANKLIN.

CANAL TRANSPORTATION

S. Rhoads, Esqr.

London, Aug' 22, 1772

DEAR FRIEND,

I THINK I before acknowledg'd your favour of Feb 29. I have since received that of May 30. I am glad my canal papers were agreable to you. If any work of that kind is set on foot in America, I think it would be saving money to engage by a handsome salary an engineer from hence who has been accustomed to such business. The many canals on foot here under different great masters, are daily raising a number of pupils in the art, some of whom may want employ hereafter; and a single mistake thro' inexperience, in such important works, may cost much more than the expence of salary to an ingenious young man already well acquainted with both principles and practice. This the Irish have learnt at a dear rate in the first attempt of their great canal, and now are endeavouring to get Smeaton to come & rectify their errors. With regard to your question, whether it is best to make the Skuylkill a part of the navigation to the back country, or whether the difficulty, of that river, subject to all the inconveniencies of floods, ice, &c will not be greater than the expence of digging, locks, &c. I can only say, that here they look on the *constant practicability* of a navigation, allowing boats to pass and repass at all times and seasons, without hindrance, to be a point of the greatest importance, and therefore they seldom or ever use a river where it can be avoided. Locks in rivers are subject to many more accidents than those in still-water canals; and the carrying away a few locks by freshes or ice, not only creates a great expence, but interrupts business for a long time till repairs are made; which may soon be destroyed again; and thus the carrying-on a course of business by such a navigation be discouraged, as subject to frequent interruptions: the toll too must be higher to pay for such repairs. Rivers are ungovernable things, especially in hilly countries: canals are quiet and very manageable: therefore they are often carried on here by the sides of rivers, only on ground above the reach of floods, no other use being made of the rivers than to supply occasionally the waste of water in the canals.

I warmly wish success to every attempt for improvement of our dear country; and am with sincere esteem,

Yours most affectionately

B. FRANKLIN

I congratulate you on the change of our American Minister. The present has more favourable dispositions towards us than his predecessor.

INDIAN CORN

IT is remark'd in North America, that the English farmers, when they first arrive there, finding the soil and climate proper for the husbandry they have been accustomed to, and particularly suitable for raising wheat, they despise and neglect the culture of mayz: but observing the advantage it affords their neighbours, the older inhabitants, they by degrees get more and more into the practice of raising it; and the face of the country shows, from time to time, that the culture of that grain goes on visibly augmenting.

The inducements are, the many different ways in which it may be prepared, so as to afford a wholesome and pleasing nourishment to men and other animals. 1st. The family can begin to make use of it before the time of full harvest; for the tender green ears, stript of their leaves, and roasted by a quick fire till the grain is brown, and eaten with a little salt or butter, are a delicacy. 2. When the grain is riper and harder, the ears, boil'd in their leaves, and eaten with butter, are also good and agreable food. The green tender grains, dried, may be kept all the year, and, mixed with green *haricots*, also dried, make at any time a pleasing dish, being first soak'd some hours in water, and then boil'd. When the grain is ripe and hard, there are also several ways of using it. One is, to soak it all night in a *lessive*, and then pound it in a large wooden mortar with a wooden pestle; the skin of each grain is by this means stript off, and the farinaceous part left whole, which, being boil'd, swells into a white soft pulp,* and eaten with milk, or with butter and sugar, is delicious. The dry grain is also sometimes ground loosely, so as to be broke into pieces of the size of rice, and being winnow'd to separate the bran, it is then boil'd and eaten with turkies or other fowls, as rice. Ground into a finer meal, they make of it by boiling a hasty-pudding, or *bouilli*, to be eaten with milk, or with butter and sugar; this resembles what the Italians call *polenta*. They make of the same meal with water and salt, a hasty cake, which, being stuck against a hoe or any flat iron, is plac'd erect before the fire, and so baked, to be used as bread. Broth is also agreably thicken'd with the same meal. They also parch it in this manner. An iron pot is fill'd with sand, and set on the fire till the sand is very hot. Two or three pounds of the grain are then thrown in, and well mix'd with the sand by stirring. Each grain bursts and throws out a white substance of twice its bigness. The sand is separated by a wire sieve, and return'd into the pot, to be again heated and repeat the operation with fresh grain. That which is parch'd is pounded to a powder in mortars. This, being sifted, will keep long for use. An Indian will travel far and subsist long on a small bag of it, taking only 6 or 8 ounces of it per day, mix'd with water.

The flour of *mayz*, mix'd with that of wheat, makes excellent bread, sweeter and more agreable than that of wheat alone. To feed horses, it is good to soak the grain 12 hours; they mash it easier with their teeth, and it yields them more nourishment. The leaves, stript off the stalks after the grain is ripe, and ty'd up in bundles when dry, are excellent forage for horses, cows, &c. The stalks, press'd like sugar-cane, yield a sweet juice, which, being fermented and distill'd, yields an excellent spirit;

* Hulled corn.

boil'd without fermentation, it affords a pleasant syrup. In Mexico, fields are sown with it thick, that multitudes of small stalks may arise, which, being cut from time to time like asparagus, are serv'd in desserts, and their sweet juice extracted in the mouth by chewing them. The meal wet is excellent food for young chickens, and the whole grain for grown fowls.

THE ARMONICA

TO

GIAMBATISTA BECCARIA

London, July 13, 1762.

REVEREND SIR,

I ONCE promised myself the pleasure of seeing you at *Turin;* but as that is not now likely to happen, being just about returning to my native country, *America,* I sit down to take leave of you (among others of my *European* friends that I cannot see) by writing.

I thank you for the honourable mention you have so frequently made of me in your letters to Mr. *Collinson* and others, for the generous defence you undertook and executed with so much success, of my electrical opinions; and for the valuable present you have made me of your new work, from which I have received great information and pleasure. I wish I could in return entertain you with any thing new of mine on that subject; but I have not lately pursued it. Nor do I know of any one here, that is at present much engaged in it.

Perhaps, however, it may be agreeable to you, as you live in a musical country, to have an account of the new instrument lately added here to the great number that charming science was before possessed of: As it is an instrument that seems peculiarly adapted to *Italian* music, especially that of the soft and plaintive kind, I will endeavour to give you such a description of it, and of the manner of constructing it, that you, or any of your friends may be enabled to imitate it, if you incline so to do, without being at the expence and trouble of the many experiments I have made in endeavouring to bring it to its present perfection.

You have doubtless heard the sweet tone that is drawn from a drinking-glass, by passing a wet finger round its brim. One Mr. *Puckeridge*, a gentleman from *Ireland*, was the first who thought of playing tunes, formed of these tones. He collected a number of glasses of different sizes, fixed them near each other on a table, and tuned them by putting into them water, more or less, as each note required. The tones were brought out by passing his fingers round their brims. He was unfortunately burnt here, with his instrument, in a fire which consumed the house he lived in. Mr. E. *Delaval*, a most ingenious member of our Royal Society, made one in imitation of it, with a better choice and form of glasses, which was the first I saw or heard. Being charmed by the sweetness of its tones, and the music he produced from it, I wished only to see the glasses disposed in a more convenient form, and brought together in a narrower compass, so as to admit of a greater number of tunes, and all within reach of hand to a person sitting before the instrument, which I accomplished, after various intermediate trials, and less commodious forms, both of glasses and construction, in the following manner.

The glasses are blown as near as possible in the form of hemispheres, having each an open neck or socket in the middle. (See Plate, Figure 1.) The thickness of the glass near the brim about a tenth of an inch, or hardly quite so much, but thicker as it comes nearer the neck, which in the largest glasses is about an

fig. 1

fig. 2

THE ARMONICA

inch deep, and an inch and half wide within, these dimensions lessening as the glasses themselves diminish in size, except that the neck of the smallest ought not to be shorter than half an inch. The largest glass is nine inches diameter, and the smallest three inches. Between these there are twenty-three different sizes, differing from each other a quarter of an inch in diameter. To make a single instrument there should be at least six glasses blown of each size; and out of this number one may probably pick 37 glasses, (which are sufficient for three octaves with all the semitones) that will be each either the note one wants or a little sharper than that note, and all fitting so well into each other as to taper pretty regularly from the largest to the smallest. It is true there are not 37 sizes, but it often happens that two of the same size differ a note or half note in tone, by reason of a difference in thickness, and these may be placed one in the other without sensibly hurting the regularity of the taper form.

The glasses being chosen and every one marked with a diamond the note you intend it for, they are to be tuned by diminishing the thickness of those that are too sharp. This is done by grinding them round from the neck towards the brim, the breadth of one or two inches, as may be required; often trying the glass by a well-tuned harpsichord, comparing the tone drawn from the glass by your finger, with the note you want, as sounded by that string of the harpsichord. When you come near the matter, be careful to wipe the glass clean and dry before each trial, because the tone is something flatter when the glass is wet, than it will be when dry; and grinding a very little between each trial, you will thereby tune to great exactness. The more care is necessary in this, because if you go below your required tone, there is no sharpening it again but by grinding somewhat off the brim which will afterwards require polishing, and thus encrease the trouble.

The glasses being thus tuned, you are to be provided with a case for them, and a spindle on which they are to be fixed. (See Plate, Figure 2.) My case is about three feet long, eleven inches every way wide within at the biggest end, and five inches at the smallest end; for it tapers all the way, to adapt it better to the conical figure of the set of glasses. This case opens in the middle of its height, and the upper part turns up by hinges fixed behind. The spindle which is of hard iron, lies horizontally from end to end of the box within, exactly in the middle, and is made to turn on brass gudgeons at each end. It is round, an inch diameter at the thickest end, and tapering to a quarter of an inch at the smallest. A square shank comes from its thickest end through the box, on which shank a wheel is fixed by a screw. This wheel serves as a fly to make the motion equable, when the spindle, with the glasses, is turned by the foot like a spinning-wheel. My wheel is of mahogany, 18 inches diameter, and pretty thick, so as to conceal near its circumference about 25 lb of lead. An ivory pin is fixed in the face of this wheel, and about 4 inches from the axis. Over the neck of this pin is put the loop of the string that comes up from the moveable step to give it motion. The case stands on a neat frame with four legs.

To fix the glasses on the spindle, a cork is first to be fitted in each neck pretty tight, and projecting a little without the neck, that the neck of one may not touch the inside of another when put together, for that would make a jarring. These corks are to be perforated with holes of different diameters, so as to suit that part of the spindle on which they are to be fixed. When a glass is put on, by holding it stiffly between both hands, while another turns the spindle, it may be gradually brought to its place. But care must be taken that the hole be not too small, lest, in forcing it up the neck should split; not too large, lest the glass, not being firmly fixed, should turn or move on the spindle, so as to touch and jar against its neighboring glass. The glasses thus are placed one in another, the largest on the biggest end of the spindle which is to the left hand; the neck of this glass is towards the wheel, and the next goes into it in the same position, only about an inch of its brim appearing beyond the brim of the first; thus proceeding, every glass when fixed shows about an inch of its brim (or three quarters of an inch, or half an inch, as they grow smaller) beyond the brim of the glass that contains it; and it is from these exposed parts of each glass that the tone is drawn, by laying a finger upon one of them as the spindle and glasses turn round.

My largest glass is G, a little below reach of a common voice, and my highest G, including three compleat octaves. To distinguish the glasses the more readily to the eye, I have painted the apparent parts of the glasses within side, every semitone white, and the other notes of the octaves with the seven prismatic colours, *viz.* C, red; D, orange; E, yellow; F, green; G, blue; A, indigo; B, purple; and C, red again; so that glasses of the same colour (the white excepted) are always octaves to each other.

This instrument is played upon, by sitting before the middle of the set of glasses as before the keys of a harpsichord, turning them with the foot, and wetting them now and then with a spunge and clean water. The fingers should be first a little soaked in water, and quite free from all greasiness; a little fine chalk upon them is sometimes useful, to make them catch the glass and bring out the tone more readily. Both hands are used, by which means different parts are played together. Observe, that the tones are best drawn out when the glasses turn *from* the ends of the fingers, not when they turn *to* them.

The advantages of this instrument are, that its tones are incomparably sweet beyond those of any other; that they may be swelled and softened at pleasure by stronger or weaker pressures of the finger, and continued to any length; and that the instrument, being once well tuned, never again wants tuning.

In honour of your musical language, I have borrowed from it the name of this instrument, calling it the Armonica.

With great esteem and respect, I am, &c.

B. FRANKLIN.

DIVERS EXPERIMENTS
and OBSERVATIONS

FIRST HYDROGEN BALLOON

SIR JOSEPH BANKS

Passy, Aug. 30, 1783.

SIR,

O N Wednesday the 27th instant, the new aerostatic experiment, invented by Messrs. Mongolfier of Annonay
was repeated by Mr. Charles; Professor of Experimental Philosophy at Paris.

A hollow globe 12 feet diameter was formed of what is called
in England oiled silk, here Taffetas *gommée*, the silk being im-
pregnated with a solution of gum-elastic in lintseed oil, as is
said. The parts were sewed together while wet with the gum,
and some of it was afterwards passed over the seams, to render
it as tight as possible.

It was afterwards filled with the inflammable air that is produced by pouring oil of vitriol upon filings of iron, when it was
found to have a tendency upwards so strong as to be capable of
lifting a weight of 39 pounds, exclusive of its own weight which
was 25 lb. and the weight of the air contain'd.

It was brought early in the morning to the *Champ de Mars,*
a field in which reviews are sometimes made, lying between the
Military School and the river. There it was held down by a
cord, till 5 in the afternoon, when it was to be let loose. Care

was taken before the hour to replace what portion had been lost of the inflammable air, or of its force, by injecting more.

It is supposed that not less than 50,000 people were assembled to see the experiment. The Champ de Mars being surrounded by multitudes, and vast numbers on the opposite side of the river.

At 5 o clock notice was given to the spectators by the firing of two cannons, that the cord was about to be cut. And presently the globe was seen to rise, and that as fast as a body of 12 feet diameter with a force only of 39 pounds, could be suppos'd to move the resisting air out of its way. There was some wind, but not very strong. A little rain had wet it, so that it shone, and made an agreeable appearance. It diminished in apparent magnitude as it rose, till it enter'd the clouds, when it seem'd to me scarce bigger than an orange, and soon after became invisible, the clouds concealing it.

The multitude separated, all well satisfied & much delighted with the success of the experiment, and amusing one another with discourses of the various uses it may possibly be apply'd to, among which many were very extravagant. But possibly it may pave the way to some discoveries in natural philosophy of which at present we have no conception.

A note secur'd from the weather had been affix'd to the globe, signifying the time & place of its departure, and praying those who might happen to find it, to send an account of its state to certain persons at Paris. No news was heard of it till the next day, when information was receiv'd, that it fell a little after 6 oclock at Gonesse, a place about 4 leagues distance; and that it was rent open, and some say had ice in it. It is suppos'd to have burst by the elasticity of the contain'd air when no longer compress'd by so heavy an atmosphere.

One of 38 feet diameter is preparing by M. Mongolfier himself at the expence of the Academy, which is to go up in a few days. I am told it is constructed of linen & paper, and is to be filled with a different air, not yet made public, but cheaper than that produc'd by the oil of vitriol of which 200 Paris pints were consum'd in filling the other.

It is said that for some days after its being fill'd, the ball was found to lose an eighth part of its force of levity in 24 hours: Whether this was from imperfection in the tightness of the ball, or a change in the nature of the air, experiments may easily discover.

I thought it my duty, Sir, to send any early account of this extraordinary fact, to the Society which does me the honour to reckon me among its members; and I will endeavor to make it more perfect, as I receive farther information.

> *With great respect, I am, Sir,*
>
> [B. FRANKLIN.]

P.S.

.   .   .   .

I just now learn, that some observers say, the ball was 150 seconds in rising, from the cutting of the cord till hid in the clouds; that its height was then about 500 toises, but, mov'd out of the perpendicular by the wind, it had made a slant so as to form a triangle, whose base on the earth was about 200 toises. It is said the country people who saw it fall were frightened, conceiv'd from its bounding a little when it touch'd the ground, that there was some living animal in it, and attack'd it with stones and knives, so that it was much mangled; but it is now brought to town & will be repaired.

The great one of M. Mongolfier, is to go up as is said, from Versailles, in about 8 or 10 days. It is not a globe but of a different form, more convenient for penetrating the air. It contains 50,000 cubic feet, and is supposed to have a force of levity equal to 1500 pounds weight. A philosopher here, M. Pilatre de Rozier, has seriously apply'd to the Academy for leave to go up with it, in order to make some experiments. He was complimented on his zeal and courage for the promotion of science, but advis'd to wait till the management of these balls was made by experience more certain & safe. They say the filling of it in M. Mongolfier's way will not cost more than half a crown. One is talk'd of to be 110 feet diameter. Several gentlemen have ordered small ones to be made for their amusement; one has ordered four of 15 feet diameter each; I know not with what purpose; but such is the present enthusiasm for promoting & improving this discovery, that probably we shall soon make considerable progress in the art of constructing and using the machines:—

Among the pleasantries conversation produces on this subject, some suppose flying to be now invented, and that since men may be supported in the air, nothing is wanted but some light handy instruments to give and direct motion. Some think progressive motion on the earth may be advanc'd by it, and that a running footman or a horse slung & suspended under such a globe so as to leave no more of weight pressing the earth with their feet, than perhaps 8 or 10 pounds, might with a fair wind run in a straight line across countries as fast as that wind, and over hedges, ditches, & even waters. It has been even fancied that in time people will keep such globes anchored in the air, to which by pullies they may draw up game to be preserved in the cool, & water to be frozen when ice is wanted. And that to get money, it will be contrived to give people an extensive view of the country, by running them upon an elbow chair a mile high for a guinea, &c. &c.

A HOT-AIR BALLOON

TO

SIR JOSEPH BANKS

Passy, Oct. 8, 1783

SIR,

THE publick were promis'd a printed particular account of the rise & progress of the balloon invention, to be publish'd about the end of last month. I waited for it, to send it to you expecting it would be more satisfactory than any thing I could write; but it does not yet appear. We have only at present the enclos'd pamphlet which does not answer the expectation given us. I send you with it some prints. That of the balloon rais'd at Versailles is said to be an exact representation. I was not present, but am told it was fill'd in about ten minutes by means of burning straw. Some say water was thrown into the flame, others that it was spirits of sal volatile. It was suppos'd to have risen about 200 toises: but did not continue long at that height, was carried horizontally by the wind and descended gently as the air within grew cooler. So vast a bulk when it began to rise so majestically in the air, struck the spectators with surprise and admiration. The basket contain'd a sheep, a duck & a cock, who except the cock receiv'd no hurt by the fall.

The Duke de Crillon made a feast last week in the Bois de Boulogne just by my habitation, on occasion of the birth of two

[94]

Spanish princes. After the fireworks, we had a balloon of about 5 feet diameter, fill'd with permanent inflammable air. It was dismiss'd about one o'clock in the morning. It carried under it a large lanthorn with inscriptions on its sides. The night was quite calm and clear, so that it went right up. The appearance of the light diminsh'd gradually till it appear'd no bigger than one of the stars, and in about 20 minutes I lost sight of it entirely. It fell the next day on the other side of the same wood near the village Boulogne, about half after 12, having been suspended in the air 11 hours and a half. It lodg'd in a tree, and was torn in getting it down; so that it cannot be ascertain'd whether it burst when above or not, tho' that is suppos'd. Smaller repetitions of the experiment are making every day in all quarters. Some of the larger balloons that have been up, are preparing to be sent up again, in a few days; but I do not hear of any material improvements yet made either in the mechanical or chemical parts of the operation. Most is expected from the new one undertaken upon subscription by Messieurs Charles & Robert, who are men of science and mechanical dexterity. It is to carry up a man. I send you enclos'd the proposals, which it is said are already subscribed to by a considerable number, and likely to be carried into execution. If I am well at the time, I purpose to be present, being a subscriber myself, and shall send you an exact account of particulars.

. . . .

FIRST AERIAL VOYAGE BY MAN

TO

Sir Joseph Banks

*Passy, Nov. 21, 1783**

DEAR SIR,

I received your friendly letter of the 7th inst. I am glad my letters respecting the aerostatic experiment were not unacceptable. But as more perfect accounts of the construction and management of that machine have been and will be publish'd before your transactions, and from which extracts may be made that will be more particular & therefore more satisfactory, I think it best not to print those letters. I say this in answer to your question for I did not indeed write them with a view of their being inserted. M. Faujas de St. Fond acquainted me yesterday, that a book on the subject which has been long expected, will be publish'd in a few days, and I shall send you one of them. Enclos'd is a copy of the *Proces verbal* taken of the experiment made yesterday in the garden of the queen's palace la Muette where the Dauphin now resides, which being near my house I was present. This paper was drawn up hastily, & may in some places appear to you obscure; therefore I shall add a few explanatory observations.

This balloon was larger than that which went up from Versailles, and carried the sheep, &c. Its bottom was open, and in

* This letter should be dated November 22, inasmuch as d'Arlandes and de Rozier made the ascension on November 21.

the middle of the opening was fix'd a kind of basket grate in which faggots and sheaves of straw were burnt. The air rarified in passing thro' this flame rose in the ballon, swell'd out its sides & fill'd it.

The persons who were plac'd in the gallery made of wicker, and attach'd to the outside near the bottom, had each of them a port thro' which they could pass sheaves of straw into the grate to keep up the flame, & thereby keep the balloon full. When it went over our heads, we could see the fire which was very considerable. As the flame slackens, the rarified air cools and condenses, the bulk of the balloon diminishes and it begins to descend. If these in the gallery see it likely to descend in an improper place they can, by throwing on more straw, & renewing the flame, make it rise again, and the wind carries it further.

La Machine poussé par le Vent s'est dirigée sur une des Allées du Jardin. That is, against the trees of one of the walks. The gallery hitch'd among the top boughs of those trees which had been cut and were stiff, while the body of the balloon lean'd beyond & seem'd likely to overset. I was then in great pain for the men, thinking them in danger of being thrown out, or burnt; for I expected that the ballon being no longer upright, the flame would have laid hold of the inside that lean'd over it. But by means of some cords that were still attach'd to it, it was soon brought upright again, made to descend, & carried back to its place. It was however much damag'd.

Planant sur l'Horizon. When they were as high as they chose to be, they made less flame, and suffer'd the machine to drive horizontally with the wind, of which however they felt very little, as they went with it, and as fast. They say they had a charming view of Paris & its environs, the course of the river,

&c. but that they were once lost, not knowing what part they were over, till they saw the Dome of the Invalids, which rectified their ideas. Probably while they were employ'd in keeping up the fire, the machine might turn, and by that means they were *desorienté* as the French call it.

There was a vast concourse of gentry in the garden, who had great pleasure in seeing the adventurers go off so chearfully, & applauded them by clapping, &c. but there was at the same time a good deal of anxiety for their safety. Multitudes in Paris saw the balloon passing; but did not know there were men with it, it being then so high that they could not see them.

Developant du Gaz. That is, in plain English, *burning more straw;* for tho' there is a little mystery made, concerning the kind of air with which the balloon is fill'd I conceive it to be nothing more than hot smoke or common air rarify'd, — tho' in this I may be mistaken;—

Ayant encore dans leur Galerie le deux tiers de leur approvisionment. That is, their provision of straw; of which they carried up a great quantity. It was well that in the hurry of so hazardous an experiment, the flame did not happen by any accidental mismanagement to lay hold of this straw; tho' each had a bucket of water by him, by way of precaution.

One of these courageous philosophers, the Marquis d'Arlandes, did me the honour to call upon me in the evening after the experiment with Mr. Mongolfier the very ingenious inventor. I was happy to see him safe. He inform'd me they lit gently without the least shock, and the balloon was very little damag'd.

. . . .

B. FRANKLIN.

[98]

SECOND AERIAL VOYAGE BY MAN

TO

SIR JOSEPH BANKS

Passy, Dec. 1, 1783.

DEAR SIR:—

IN mine of yesterday I promised to give you an account of Messrs. Charles & Robert's experiment, which was to have been made this day, and at which I intended to be present. Being a little indisposed, and the air cool, and the ground damp, I declined going into the garden of the Tuileries, where the balloon was placed, not knowing how long I might be obliged to wait there before it was ready to depart, and chose to stay in my carriage near the statue of Louis XV., from whence I could well see it rise, and have an extensive view of the region of air through which, as the wind sat, it was likely to pass. The morning was foggy, but about one o'clock the air became tolerably clear, to the great satisfaction of the spectators, who were infinite, notice having been given of the intended experiment several days before in the papers, so that all Paris was out, either about the Tuileries, on the quays and bridges, in the fields, the streets, at the windows, or on the tops of houses, besides the inhabitants of all the towns and villages of the environs. Never before was a philosophical experiment so magnificently attended. Some guns were fired to give notice that the departure of the balloon was near, and a small one was discharged, which went to an amazing height, there being but little wind to make it deviate from its perpendicular course, and at length the sight of it was lost. Means were used, I am told, to prevent the great balloon's rising so high as might endanger its bursting. Several bags of sand were taken on board before the cord that held it down was cut, and the whole weight being then too much to be lifted, such a quantity was discharged as to permit its rising slowly. Thus it would sooner arrive at that region where it would be in equilibrio with the surrounding air, and by discharging more sand afterwards, it might go higher if desired. Between one and two o'clock, all eyes were gratified with seeing it rise majestically from among the trees, and ascend gradually above the buildings, a most beautiful spectacle. When it was about two hundred feet high, the brave adventurers held out and waved a little white pennant, on both sides their car, to salute the spectators, who returned loud claps of applause. The wind was very little, so that the object though moving to the northward, continued long in view; and it was a great while before the admiring people began to disperse. The persons embarked were Mr. Charles, professor of experimental philosophy, and a zealous promoter of that science; and one of the Messieurs Robert, the very ingenious constructors of the machine. When it arrived at its height, which I suppose might be three or four hundred toises, it appeared to have only horizontal motion. I had a pocket-glass, with which I followed it, till I lost sight first of the men, then of the car, and when I last saw the balloon, it appeared no bigger than a walnut. I write this at seven in the evening. What became of them is not yet known here. I hope they descended by daylight, so as to see and avoid falling among trees or on houses, and that the experiment was completed without any mischievous accident, which the novelty of it and the want of experience might well occasion. I am the more anxious for the event, because I am not well informed of the means provided for letting themselves down, and the loss of these very ingenious men would not only be a discouragement to the progress of the art, but be a sensible loss to science and society.

I shall inclose one of the tickets of admission, on which the globe was represented, as originally intended, but is altered by the pen to show its real state when it went off. When the tickets were engraved the car was to have been hung to the neck of the globe, as represented by a little drawing I have made in the corner.

I suppose it may have been an apprehension of danger in straining too much the balloon or tearing the silk, that induced the constructors to throw a net over it, fixed to a hoop which went round its middle, and to hang the car to that hoop.

Tuesday morning, December 2d. — I am relieved from my anxiety by hearing that the adventurers descended well near L'Isle Adam before sunset. This place is near seven leagues from Paris. Had the wind blown fresh they might have gone much farther.

If I receive any further particulars of importance, I shall communicate them hereafter.

With great esteem, I am, dear sir, your most obedient and most humble servant,

B. FRANKLIN.

P.S. *Tuesday evening.*— Since writing the above I have received the printed paper and the manuscript containing some particulars of the experiment, which I enclose. I hear further that the travellers had perfect command of their carriage, descending as they pleased by letting some of the inflammable air escape, and rising again by discharging some sand; that they descended over a field so low as to talk with the labourers in passing, and mounted again to pass a hill. The little balloon falling at Vincennes shows that mounting higher it met with a current of air in a contrary direction, an observation that may be of use to future aerial voyagers.

A PROPHECY ON AERIAL
NAVIGATION

TO

JAN INGENHOUSZ

Passy, Jan. 16, 1784.

DEAR FRIEND,

I HAVE this day received your favor of the 2d inst. Every information in my power, respecting the balloons, I sent you just before Christmas, contained in copies of my letters to Sir Joseph Banks. There is no secret in the affair, and I make no doubt that a person coming from you would easily obtain a sight of the different balloons of Montgolfier and Charles, with all the instructions wanted; and, if you undertake to make one, I think it extremely proper and necessary to send an ingenious man here for that purpose: otherwise, for want of attention to some particular circumstance, or of not being acquainted with it, the experiment might miscarry, which, in an affair of so much public expectation, would have bad consequences, draw upon you a great deal of censure, and affect your reputation. It is a serious thing to draw out from their affairs all the inhabitants of a great city and its environs, and a disappointment makes them angry. At Bordeaux lately a person who pretended to send up a balloon, and had received money from many people, not being able to make it rise, the populace were so exasperated that they pulled down his house, and had like to have killed him.

It appears, as you observe, to be a discovery of great importance, and what may possibly give a new turn to human affairs. Convincing sovereigns of the folly of wars may perhaps be one effect of it; since it will be impracticable for the most potent of them to guard his dominions. Five thousand balloons, capable of raising two men each, could not cost more than five ships of the line; and where is the prince who can afford so to cover his country with troops for its defence, as that ten thousand men descending from the clouds might not in many places do an infinite deal of mischief, before a force could be brought together to repel them? It is a pity that any national jealousy should, as you imagine it may, have prevented the English from prosecuting the experiment, since they are such ingenious mechanicians, that in their hands it might have made a more rapid progress towards perfection, and all the utility it is capable of affording.

The balloon of Messrs. Charles and Robert was really filled with inflamable air. The quantity being great, it was expensive, and tedious filling, requiring two or three days and nights constant labour. It had a *soupape*, [or valve,] near the top, which they could open by pulling a string and thereby let out some air when they had a mind to descend; and they discharged some of their ballast of sand when they would rise again. A great deal of air must have been let out when they landed, so that the loose part might envelope one of them: yet, the car being lightned by that one getting out of it, there was enough left to carry up the other rapidly. They had no fire with them. That is only used in M. Montgolfier's globe, which is open at bottom, and straw constantly burnt to keep it up. This kind is sooner and cheaper filled; but must be much bigger to carry up the same weight; since air rarified by heat is only twice as light as common air, and inflamable air is ten times lighter. M. de Morveau, a famous chemist at Dijon, has found an inflamable air that will cost only a 25th part of the price of what is made by oil of vitriol poured on iron filings. They say it is made from sea coal. Its comparative weight is not mentioned.

Yours most affectionately,
B. FRANKLIN.

MAGIC SQUARES

TO

PETER COLLINSON

[c. 1750]

SIR,

ACCORDING to your request, I now send you the Arithmetical Curiosity, of which this is the history.

Being one day in the country, at the house of our common friend, the late learned, Mr. *Logan,* he shewed me a folio *French* book, filled with magic squares, . . . in which he said, the author had discovered great ingenuity and dexterity in the management of numbers; and, though several other foreigners had distinguished themselves in the same way, he did not recollect that any one *Englishman* had done anything of the kind remarkable.

. . . I then confessed to him, that in my younger days, having once some leisure, (which I still think I might have employed more usefully) I had amused myself in making these kind of magic squares, and, at length, had acquired such a knack at it, that I could fill the cells of any magic square, of reasonable size, with a series of numbers as fast as I could write them, disposed in such a manner, as that the sums of every row, horizontal, perpendicular, or diagonal, should be equal; but not being satisfied with these, which I looked on as common and easy things, I had imposed on myself more difficult tasks, and succeeded in making other magic squares, with a variety of properties, and much more curious. He then shewed me several in the same book, of an uncommon and more curious kind; but, as I thought none of them equal to some I remembered to have made, he desired me to let him see them; and accordingly, the next time I visited him, I carried him a square of 8, which I found among my old papers, and which I will now give you, with an account of its properties. [See figure 1]

The properties are,

1. That every strait row (horizontal or vertical) of 8 numbers added together, makes 260, and half each row half 260.

2. That the bent row of 8 numbers, ascending and descending diagonally, *viz.* from 16 ascending to 10, and from 23 descending to 17; and every one of its parallel bent rows of 8 numbers, make 260. Also the bent row from 52, descending to 54, and from 43 ascending to 45; and every one of its parallel bent rows of 8 numbers, make 260. Also the bent row from 45 to 43

52	61	4	13	20	29	36	45
14	3	62	51	46	35	30	19
53	60	5	12	21	28	37	44
11	6	59	54	43	38	27	22
55	58	7	10	23	26	39	42
9	8	57	56	41	40	25	24
50	63	2	15	18	31	34	47
16	1	64	49	48	33	32	17

fig. 1.

descending to the left, and from 23 to 17 descending to the right, and every one of its parallel bent rows of 8 numbers, make 260. Also the bent row from 52 to 54 descending to the right, and from 10 to 16 descending to the left, and every one of its parallel bent rows of 8 numbers, make 260. Also the parallel bent rows next to the above-mentioned, which are shortened to 3 numbers ascending, and 3 descending, &c., as from 53 to 4 ascending, and from 29 to 44 descending, make, with the 2 corner numbers, 260. Also the 2 numbers, 14, 61 ascending, and 36, 19, descending, with the lower 4 numbers situated like them, *viz.* 50, 1 descending, and 32, 47, ascending, make 260. And, lastly, the 4 corner numbers, with the 4 middle numbers, make 260.

So this magical square seems perfect in its kind. But these are not all its properties; there are 5 other curious ones, which, at some other time, I will explain to you.

. . . .

. . . I went home, and made, that evening, the following magical square of 16, which, besides having all the properties of the foregoing square of eight, *i.e.* it would make the 2056 in all the same rows and diagonals, had this added, that a four square hole being cut in a piece of paper of such a size as to take in and shew through it, just 16 of the little squares, when laid on the greater square, the sum of the 16 numbers so appearing through the hole, wherever it was placed on the greater square, should likewise make 2056. This I sent to our friend the next morning, who, after some days, sent it back in a letter with these words; "I return to thee thy astonishing or most stupendous piece of the magical square, in which" — but the compliment is too extravagant, and therefore, for his sake, as well as my own, I ought not to repeat it. Nor is it necessary; for I make no question but you will readily allow this square of 16 to be the most magically magical of any magic square ever made by any magician. [See figure 2]

. . . .

B. FRANKLIN.

200	217	232	249	8	25	40	57	72	89	104	121	136	153	168	181
58	39	26	7	250	231	218	199	186	167	154	135	122	103	90	71
198	219	230	251	6	27	38	59	70	91	102	123	134	155	166	187
60	37	28	5	252	229	220	197	188	165	156	133	124	101	92	69
201	216	233	248	9	24	41	56	73	88	105	120	137	152	169	184
55	42	23	10	247	234	215	202	183	170	151	138	119	106	87	74
20	214	235	246	11	22	43	54	75	86	107	118	139	150	171	182
53	44	21	12	245	236	213	204	181	172	149	140	117	108	85	76
205	212	237	244	13	20	45	52	77	84	109	116	141	148	173	180
51	46	19	14	243	238	241	206	179	174	147	142	115	110	83	78
207	210	239	242	15	18	47	50	79	82	111	114	143	146	175	178
49	48	17	16	241	240	209	208	177	176	145	144	113	112	81	80
196	221	228	253	4	29	36	61	68	93	100	125	132	157	164	189
62	35	30	3	254	227	222	195	190	163	158	131	126	99	94	67
194	223	226	251	2	31	34	63	66	95	98	127	130	159	162	191
64	33	32	1	256	225	224	193	192	161	160	129	128	97	96	65

fig. 2

MAGIC SQUARE

EARLY ELECTRICAL EXPERIMENTS

[*Philadelphia*], 1749

SIR,

. . . .

CHAGRINED a little that we have been hitherto able to produce nothing in this way of use to mankind; and the hot weather coming on, when electrical experiments are not so agreeable, it is proposed to put an end to them for this season, somewhat humorously, in a party of pleasure on the banks of *Skuylkil.* Spirits, at the same time, are to be fired by a spark sent from side to side through the river, without any other conductor than the water; an experiment which we some time since performed, to the amazement of many.

A turkey is to be killed for our dinner by the *electrical shock,* and roasted by the *electrical jack,* before a fire kindled by the *electrified bottle:* when the healths of all the famous electricians in *England, Holland, France,* and *Germany* are to be drank in *electrified bumpers,* under the discharge of guns from the *electrical battery.*

April 29, 1749.

ELECTRICAL EXPERIMENTS

TO

JOHN LINING

at Charleston, South Carolina

Philadelphia, March 18, 1755

SIR,

·   ·   ·   ·   ·   ·   ·   ·   ·   ·   ·   ·

YOUR question, how I came first to think of proposing the experiment of drawing down the lightning, in order to ascertain its sameness with the electric fluid, I cannot answer better than by giving you an extract from the minutes I used to keep of the experiments I made, with memorandums of such as I purposed to make, the reasons for making them, and the observations that arose upon them, from which minutes my letters were afterwards drawn. By this extract you will see, that the thought was not so much "an out-of-the-way one," but that it might have occurred to any electrician.

"*November* 7, 1749. Electrical fluid agrees with lightning in these particulars. 1. Giving light. 2. Colour of the light. 3. Crooked direction. 4. Swift motion. 5. Being conducted by metals. 6. Crack or noise in exploding. 7. Subsisting in water or ice. 8. Rending bodies it passes through. 9. Destroying animals. 10. Melting metals. 11. Firing inflammable substances. 12. Sulphureous smell. The electric fluid is attracted by points. We do not know whether this property is in lightning. But since they agree in all particulars wherein we can already compare them, is it not probable they agree likewise in this? Let the experiment be made."

I wish I could give you any satisfaction in the article of clouds. I am still at a loss about the manner in which they become charged with electricity; no hypothesis I have yet formed perfectly satisfying me. Some time since, I heated very hot a brass plate, two feet square, and placed it on an electric stand. From the plate a wire extended horizontally four or five feet, and, at the end of it, hung, by linnen threads, a pair of cork balls. I then repeatedly sprinkled water over the plate, that it might be raised from it in vapour, hoping that if the vapour either carried off the electricity of the plate, or left behind it that of the water, (one of which I supposed it must do, if, like the clouds, it became electrised itself, either positively or negatively) I should perceive and determine it by the separation of the balls, and by finding whether they were positive or negative; but no alteration was made at all, nor could I perceive that the steam was itself electrised, though I have still some suspicion that the steam was not fully examined, and I think the experiment should be repeated. Whether the first state of electrised clouds is positive or negative, if I could find the cause of that, I should be at no loss about the other, for either is easily deduced from the other, as one state is easily produced by the other. A strongly positive cloud may drive out of a neighboring cloud much of its natural quantity of the electric fluid, and, passing by it, leave it in a negative state. In the same way, a strongly negative cloud may occasion a neighboring cloud to draw into itself from others an additional quantity, and, passing by it, leave it in a positive state. How these effects may be produced, you will easily conceive, on perusing and considering the experiments in the enclosed paper: And from them too it appears probable, that every change from positive to negative, and from negative to positive, that, during a thunder gust, we see in the cork-balls annexed to the apparatus, is not owing to the presence of clouds in the same state, but often to the absence of positive or negative clouds, that having just passed, leave the rod in the opposite state.

The knocking down of the six men was performed with two of my large jarrs not fully charged. I laid one end of my discharging rod upon the head of the first; he laid his hand on the head of the second; the second his hand on the head of the third, and so to the last, who held, in his hand, the chain that was connected with the outside of the jarrs. When they were thus placed, I applied the other end of my rod to the prime-conductor, and they all dropt together. When they got up, they all declared they had not felt any stroke, and wondered how they came to fall; nor did any of them either hear the crack, or see the light of it. You suppose it a dangerous experiment; but I had once suffered the same myself, receiving, by accident, an equal stroke through my head, that struck me down, without hurting me: And I had seen a young woman, that was about to be electrified through the feet, (for some indisposition) receive a greater charge through the head, by inadvertently stooping forward to look at the placing of her feet, till her forhead (as she was very tall) came too near my prime-conductor: she dropt, but instantly got up again, complaining of nothing. A person so struck, sinks down doubled, or folded together as it were, the joints losing their strength and stiffness at once, so that he drops on the spot where he stood, instantly, and there is no previous staggering, nor does he ever fall lengthwise. Too great a charge might, indeed, kill a man, but I have not yet seen any hurt done by it. It would certainly, as you observe, be the easiest of all deaths.

The experiment you have heard so imperfect an account of, is merely this. — I electrified a silver pint cann, on an electric stand, and then lowered into it a cork ball, of about an inch diameter, hanging by a silk string, till the cork touched the bottome of the cann. The cork was not attracted to the inside of the cann, as it would have been to the outside, and though it touched the bottom, yet, when drawn out, it was not found to be electrified by that touch, as it would have been by touching the outside. The fact is singular. You require the reason; I do not know it. Perhaps you may discover it, and then you will be so good as to communicate it to me.* I find a frank acknowledgement of one's ignorance is not only the easiest way to get rid of a difficulty, but the likliest way to obtain information, and therefore I practise it: I think it an honest policy. Those who affect to be thought to know every thing, and so undertake to explain every thing, often remain long ignorant of many things that others could and would instruct them in, if they appeared less conceited.

· · · · · · · · · · · ·

B. F[ranklin]

* Mr. *F.* has since thought, that possibly, the mutual repulsion of the inner opposite sides of the electrified cann, may prevent the accumulating an electric atmosphere upon them, and occasion it to stand chiefly on the outside. But recommends it to the farther examination of the curious. *F.*

THE KITE

TO

PETER COLLINSON

[*Philadelphia*] *October* 19, 1752.

SIR,

AS frequent mention is made in public papers from *Europe* of the success of the *Philadelphia* experiment for drawing the electric fire from clouds by means of pointed rods of iron erected on high buildings, &, it may be agreeable to the curious to be informed, that the same experiment has succeeded in *Philadelphia*, though made in a different and more easy manner, which is as follows:

Make a small cross of two light strips of cedar, the arms so long as to reach to the four corners of a large thin silk handkerchief when extended; tie the corners of the handkerchief to the extremities of the cross, so you have the body of a kite; which being properly accommodated with a tail, loop, and string, will rise in the air, like those made of paper; but this being of silk, is fitter to bear the wet and wind of a thunder-gust without tearing. To the top of the upright stick of the cross is to be fixed a very sharp-pointed wire, rising a foot or more above the wood. To the end of the twine, next the hand, is to be tied a silk ribbon, and where the silk and twine join, a key may be fastened. This kite is to be raised when a thunder-gust appears to be coming on, and the person who holds the string must stand within a door or window or under some cover, so that the silk ribbon may not be wet; and care must be taken that the twine does not touch the frame of the door or window. As soon as any of the thunder-clouds come over the kite, the pointed wire will draw the electric fire from them, and the kite, with all the twine, will be electrified, and the loose filaments of the twine will stand out every way, and be attracted by an approaching finger. And when the rain has wet the kite and twine, so that it can conduct the electric fire freely, you will find it stream out plentifully from the key on the approach of your knuckle. At this key the phial may charged; and from electric fire thus obtained, spirits may be kindled, and all the other electric experiments be performed, which are usually done by the help of a rubbed glass globe or tube, and thereby the sameness of the electric matter with that of lightning completely demonstrated.

B. FRANKLIN.

THE COURSE *and* EFFECT
of LIGHTNING

Philada Thursday July 12, 1753

O N Sunday last about 45 minutes after 3 in the morning a dwelling house, one of a continued row on the west side of Second street in this town, was struck by lightning, but, being at that time untenanted, no person was hurt. About 6 o'clock the same morning, I went to take a view thereof, and at that time made some notes of the course which I observed the lightning to have taken in its passage, and also of some of its effects on the house, when they appeared to me not unworthy of notice.

The course is as follows, viz.

The lightning, or matter thereof, (supposing it to have enter'd at the top of the house, as is the general receiv'd opinion,) first struck the southeast corner of the eastermost chimney; from which place it can be trac'd downwards, by cracks and other marks on the south side of the chimney, in a diagonal line, to the bottom of a kind of bulk-head, or place rais'd above the roof, to go out on the top of the house, and reaching from one chimney to the other; that it then appears to have gone up the E. side of the roof, near the edge of the S. side of the bulk-head to the ridge, and from thence descended the W. side of the roof, by the like way, to the bulkhead door, which it split, and melted part of an iron staple on the inside of the westermost side of the door-frame; that from thence its course was continued down the W. side of the roof, by the S. side of the western chimney, till it came to a place where the roof bent or flaunted downwards, along the ridge of which bent it turn'd & pass'd southward to a dormer window, flat on the top, and which projected about 3 feet from the roof, where again it turn'd, and by the upper & N. side of the dormer proceeded W. to the further end; that from thence it was conducted downwards by the leads & window-frame on the N. side of the said window to a kind of pent-house about 2 feet wide, the wooden moulding on the under side of which was much shatter'd, and a round hole made therein, as if done by a bullet fir'd from a common swivelgun; that its course was then down to the northermost window of the 2^d story, where it diffus'd itself amongst the leads, and went out at the iron window hook, that hung down from the southern side of the sd window, about a foot below the point of which it made a considerable breach in the wall, and drove the plaistering on the inside, to the opposite side of the room; that from thence it made a small crack in the wall down to a ledge (or single row of bricks projecting about 3 inches from the wall, which the bricklayers term a water table or water fall) about mid-way between the windows of the 1st & 2^d story, and from there plowing, or scooping, as it were, the outside of the wall all the way down to the upper & southermost part of the northermost window of the 2^d story, which it entirely drove into the room; that the lightning then diffus'd itself in the leads, and descended by them to the northermost window hook, from the point of which it jump'd to the upper & eastermost corner of a window over the door of a kitchen adjoining to the northermost side of the back part of the house, and fronting the south; that from thence it was conducted by leads to the lower and westermost corner of said window from which place it again jump'd across to the kitching window, at the distance of about 2 feet, making all the way a hollow in the brick wall between, as if done by a large iron scoop; that in this last window it divided itself very much, as might be seen by the leads, which were in most places melted; that from thence no traces of it appear, except just at the points of the iron hooks, fix'd to each side of the window frames, which were about 2 feet from the ground, to where it might have been conducted by the moisture on the walls, which was very considerable, there having a great quantity of rain fell the night before.

Observation of the Effects

1. That the large black cloud, from whence the fire is generally thought to have issued, came from the southwest, yet the chimney on the back part or W. side of the house, tho' equal in heighth to that on the front or East side, and but about 9 feet distance, was not at all affected; its first appearance upwards, as mention'd before, being on the S.E. corner of the eastermost chimney.

2. That the under part of one of the bricks in a small ledge that went round the chimney, about a foot from the top, had a piece knock'd out of it, as if done by a blow of a hammer, or some other force from underneath; the bottom of the fraction being the whole breadth of the ledge, and the upper part terminating to a sharp edge, as is represented in the margin; the upper side of the ledge was no otherways hurt than but by a small crack proceeding from the fracture underneath; and the lightning appears, as if by the resistance it met with from the ledge,

to have been forc'd into the chimney, thro' the mortar between the ledge and the brick underneath.

3. That the east side of the roof, up which the fire must have pass'd, supposing it to have enter'd from above, was noways damag'd, except just at the ridge, where the thin edge of the shingles appear'd to have been thrown up by it; — but the thick end of the shingles lay perfectly close from the bottom of the eastermost chimney to the ridge, as did all those on the E. side of the roof.

4. That on the west side of the roof, quite from the extreme end of the dormer window to the ridge, in the track before described, the thick ends of the shingles are all thrown upwards, as if done by some instrument forc'd underneath them.

5. That the splinters near the hole in the wooden moulding of the under part of the pent house, before described, were all drove upwards, as if occasion'd by a bullet being shot against it from below.

6. That several of the upright parts of the window frames were, in many places, much shattered; and all the pieces that were split or torn off from them were broadest at the bottom, and terminating almost to a point at the top; whereas the contrary might have been expected to have happen'd, if the force which split them came from above.

7. That the under side of the ledge or water-table between the 1st & 2d storys, was considerably more damag'd than the upper, and a piece drove out of it, as in the ledge near the top of the chimney.

8. That the lightning went considerably out of its nearest way (supposing it to have proceeded either from above or below) for the sake of the leads of the windows, and iron hooks,

staples &c. of the window-frames; which were all much melted and stain'd thereby. Several panes of glass were also a little melted and appear'd somewhat colour'd round the edges, near where the leads surrounded it, and those parts of the leads thin, and not sufficient to conduct the whole of the flash, were melted; but the thick parts of the leads (which separate the parts from each other) conducted it freely, and without being the least damag'd.

CHARACTER *of* CLOUDS

TO

THOMAS RONAYNE

London, April 20, 1766.

SIR,

I HAVE received your very obliging and very ingenious letter by Captain Kearney. Your observations upon the electricity of fogs and the air in Ireland, and upon different circumstances of storms, appear to me very curious, and I thank
you for them. There is not, in my opinion, any part of the earth
whatever which is, or can be, naturally in a state of negative
electricity; and, though different circumstances may occasion
an inequality in the distribution of the fluid, the equilibrium is
immediately restored by means of its extreme subtilty, and of
the excellent conductors with which the humid earth is amply
provided. I am of opinion, however, that when a cloud, well
charged positively, passes near the earth, it repels and forces
down into the earth that natural portion of electricity, which
exists near its surface, and in buildings, trees, &c., so as actually
to reduce them to a negative state before it strikes them. I am
of opinion, too, that the negative state in which you have frequently found the balls, which are suspended from your apparatus, is not always occasioned by clouds in a negative state; but
more commonly by clouds positively electrified, which have
passed over them, and which in their passage have repelled and

driven off a part of the electrical matter, which naturally existed in the apparatus; so that, what remained after the passing of the clouds diffusing itself uniformly through the apparatus, the whole became reduced to a negative state.

If you have read my experiments made in continuation of those of Mr. Canton, you will readily understand this; but you may easily make a few experiments, which will clearly demonstrate it. Let a common glass be warmed before the fire, that it may continue very dry for some time; set it upon a table, and place upon it the small box made use of by Mr. Canton, so that the balls may hang a little beyond the edge of the table. Rub another glass, which has previously been warmed in a similar manner, with a piece of black silk, or a silk handkerchief, in order to electrify it. Hold then the glass above the little box, at about the distance of three or four inches from that part, which is most distant from the balls; and you will see the balls separate from each other; being positively electrified by the natural portion of electricity, which was in the box, and which is driven to the further part of it by the repulsive power of the atmosphere in the excited glass. Touch the box near the little balls (the excited glass continuing in the same state) and the balls will again unite; the quantity of electricity which had been driven to this part being drawn off by your finger. Withdraw then both your finger and the glass, at the same instant, and the quantity of electricity which remained in the box, uniformly diffusing itself, the balls will again be separated, being now in a negative state. While things are in this situation, begin once more to excite your glass, and hold it above the box, but not too near, and you will find, that, when it is brought within a certain distance, the balls will at first approach each other, being then in a natural state. In proportion as the glass is brought nearer, they will again separate, being positive. When the glass is moved beyond them, and at some little farther distance, they will unite again, being in a natural state. When it is entirely removed, they will separate again, being then made negative. The excited glass in this experiment may represent a cloud positively charged, which you see is capable of producing in this manner all the different changes in the apparatus, without the least necessity for supposing any negative cloud.

I am nevertheless fully convinced, that there are negative clouds; because they sometimes absorb, through the medium of the apparatus, the positive electricity of a large jar, the hundredth part of which the apparatus itself would have not been able to receive or contain at once. In fact, it is not difficult to conceive that a large cloud, highly charged positively, may reduce smaller clouds to a negative state, when it passes above or near them, by forcing a part of their natural portion of the fluid either to their inferior surfaces, whence it may strike into the earth, or to the opposite side, whence it may strike into the adjacent clouds; so that, when the large cloud has passed off to a distance, the small clouds shall remain in a negative state, exactly like the apparatus; the former (like the latter) being frequently insulated bodies, having communication neither with the earth nor with other clouds. Upon the same principle it may easily be conceived in what manner a large negative cloud may render others positive.

·   ·   ·   ·   ·   ·   ·   ·   ·   ·   ·

B. FRANKLIN.

MUSICAL SOUNDS

TO

LORD KAMES

Craven Street, London, June 2, 1765

MY DEAR LORD,

. . . .

GIVE me leave on this occasion to extend a little the sense of your position, that "Melody and Harmony are separately agreeable, and in union delightful," and to give it as my opinion, that the reason why the Scotch tunes have lived so long, and will probably live for ever (if they escape being stifled in modern affected ornament), is merely this, that they are really compositions of melody and harmony united, or rather that their melody is harmony. I mean the simple tunes sung by a single voice. As this will appear paradoxical, I must explain my meaning. In common acceptation, indeed, only an agreeable *succession* of sounds is called *Melody,* and only the *co-existence* of agreeing sounds, *Harmony.* But, since the memory is capable of retaining for some moments a perfect idea of the pitch of a past sound, so as to compare with it the pitch of a succeeding sound, and judge truly of their agreement or disagreement, there may and does arise from thence a sense of harmony between the present and past sounds, equally pleasing with that between two present sounds.

Now the construction of the old Scotch tunes is this, that almost every succeeding *emphatical* note is a third, a fifth, an octave, or in short some note that is in concord with the preceding note. Thirds are chiefly used, which are very pleasing concords. I use the word *emphatical* to distinguish those notes which have a stress laid on them in singing the tune, from the lighter connecting notes, that serve merely, like grammar articles, to tack the others together.

That we have a most perfect idea of a sound just past, I might appeal to all acquainted with music, who know how easy it is to repeat a sound in the same pitch with one just heard. In tuning an instrument, a good ear can as easily determine that two strings are in unison by sounding them separately, as by sounding them together; their disagreement is also as easily, I believe I may say more easily and better distinguished, when sounded separately; for when sounded together, though you know by the beating that one is higher than the other, you cannot tell which it is. I have ascribed to memory the ability of comparing the pitch of a present tone with that of one past. But, if there should be, as possibly there may be, something in the ear, similar to what we find in the eye, that ability would not be entirely owing to memory. Possibly the vibrations given to the auditory nerves by a particular sound may actually continue some time after the cause of those vibrations is past, and the agreement or disagreement of a subsequent sound become by comparison with them more discernible. For the impression made on the visual nerves by a luminous object will continue for twenty or thirty seconds. Sitting in a room, look earnestly at the middle of a window a little while when the day is bright, and then shut your eyes; the figure of the window will still remain in the eye, and so distinct that you may count the panes.

A remarkable circumstance attending this experiment, is, that the impression of forms is better retained than that of colors; for after the eyes are shut, when you first discern the image of the window, the panes appear dark, and the cross bars of the sashes, with the window frames and walls, appear white or bright; but, if you still add to the darkness in the eyes by covering them with your hand, the reverse instantly takes place, the panes appear luminous and the cross bars dark. And by removing the hand they are again reversed. This I know not how to account for. Nor for the following; that, after looking long through green spectacles, the white paper of a book will on first taking them off appear to have a blush of red; and, after long looking through red glasses, a greenish cast; this seems to intimate a relation between green and red not yet explained.

Farther, when we consider by whom these ancient tunes were composed, and how they were first performed, we shall see that such harmonical succession of sounds was natural and even necessary in their construction. They were composed by the minstrels of those days to be played on the harp accompanied by the voice. The harp was strung with wire, [which gives a sound of long continuance,] and had no contrivance, like that in the modern harpsichord, by which the sound of the preceding could be stoppt, the moment a succeeding note began. To avoid *actual* discord, it was therefore necessary that the succeeding emphatic note should be a chord with the preceding, as their sounds must exist at the same time. Hence arose that beauty in those tunes that has so long pleased, and will please for ever, though men scarce know why. That they were originally composed for the harp, and of the most simple kind, I mean a harp without any half notes but those in the natural scale, and with no more than two octaves of strings, from C to C, I conjecture from another circumstance, which is, that not one of those tunes, really ancient, has a single artificial half note in it, and that in tunes where it was most convenient for the voice to use the middle notes of the harp, and place the key in F, there the B, which if used should be a B flat, is always omitted by passing over it with a third. The connoisseurs in modern music will say, I have no taste; but I cannot help adding, that I believe our ancestors, in hearing a good song, distinctly articulated, sung to one of those tunes, and accompanied by the harp, felt more real pleasure than is communicated by the generality of modern operas, exclusive of that arising from the scenery and dancing. Most tunes of late composition, not having this natural harmony united with their melody, have recourse to the artificial harmony of a bass, and other accompanying parts. This support, in my opinion, the old tunes do not need, and are rather confused than aided by it. Whoever has heard James Oswald play them on his violoncello, will be less inclined to dispute this with me. I have more than once seen tears of pleasure in the eyes of his auditors; and yet, I think, even *his* playing those tunes would please more, if he gave them less modern ornament. My son, when we parted, desired me to present his affectionate respects to you, Lady Kames, and your amiable children: *be so good with those, to accept mine, and believe me, with sincerest esteem, my dear Lord, &c.*

B. FRANKLIN

LOCATING THE GULF STREAM

TO

DAVID LE ROY

At sea, on board the London Packet,
Capt. Truxton, August 1785.

SIR,

.   .   .   .

VESSELS are sometimes retarded, and sometimes forwarded in their voyages, by currents at sea, which are often not perceived. About the year 1769 or 70, there was an application made by the Board of Customs at Boston, to the Lords of the Treasury in London, complaining that the packets between Falmouth and New York were generally a fortnight longer in their passages, than merchant ships from London to Rhode Island, and proposing that for the future they should be ordered to Rhode Island instead of New York. Being then concerned in the management of the American post-office, I happened to be consulted on the occasion; and it appearing strange to me, that there should be such a difference between two places scarce a day's run asunder, especially when the merchant ships are generally deeper laden, and more weakly manned than the packets, and had from London the whole length of the river and channel to run before they left the land of England, while the packets had only to go from Falmouth, I could not but think the fact misunderstood or misrepresented.

[129]

There happened then to be in London a Nantucket sea captain of my acquaintance, to whom I communicated the affair. He told me he believed the fact might be true; but the difference was owing to this, that the Rhode Island captains were acquainted with the Gulf Stream, which those of the English packets were not. "We are well acquainted with that stream," says he, "because in our pursuit of whales, which keep near the sides of it, but are not to be met with in it, we run down along the sides, and frequently cross it to change our side; and in crossing it have sometimes met and spoke with those packets, who were in the middle of it, and stemming it. We have informed them that they were stemming a current, that was against them to the value of three miles an hour; and advised them to cross it and get out of it; but they were too wise to be counselled by simple American fishermen. When the winds are but light," he added, "they are carried back by the current more than they are forwarded by the wind; and, if the wind be good, the subtraction of seventy miles a day from their course is of some importance." I then observed it was a pity no notice was taken of this current upon the charts, and requested him to mark it out for me, which he readily complied with, adding directions for avoiding it in sailing from Europe to North America. . . .

This stream is probably generated by the great accumulation of water on the eastern coast of America between the tropics, by the trade winds which constantly blow there. It is known, that a large piece of water ten miles broad and generally only three feet deep, has by a strong wind had its waters driven to one side and sustained so as to become six feet deep, while the windward side was laid dry. This may give some idea of the quantity heaped up on the American coast, and the reason of its running down in a strong current through the islands into the bay of Mexico, and from thence issuing through the Gulph of Florida, and proceeding along the coast to the banks of Newfoundland, where it turns off towards and runs down through the Western Islands. Having since crossed this stream several times in passing between America and Europe, I have been attentive to sundry circumstances relating to it, by which to know when one is in it; and besides the gulf weed with which it is interspersed, I find, that it is always warmer than the sea on each side of it, and that it does not sparkle in the night. I annex hereto the observations made with the thermometer in two voyages, and possibly may add a third.* It will appear from them, that the thermometer may be a useful instrument to a navigator, since currents coming from the northward into southern seas will probably be found colder than the water of those seas, as the currents from southern seas into northern are found warmer. And it is not to be wondered, that so vast a body of deep warm water, several leagues wide, coming from between the tropics and issuing out of the gulph into the northern seas, should retain its warmth longer than the twenty or thirty days required to its passing the banks of Newfoundland. The quantity is too great, and it is too deep to be suddenly cooled by passing under a cooler air. The air immediately over it, however, may receive so much warmth from it as to be rarefied and rise, being rendered lighter than the air on each side of the stream; hence those airs must flow in to supply the place of the rising warm air, and meeting with

* The "Observations of the Warmth of the Sea Water, &c., by Fahrenheit's Thermometer . . ." may be found in the Smyth edition of Franklin's Writings, volume IX, pp. 407–411.

each other, form those tornados and waterspouts frequently met with, and seen near and over the stream; and as the vapour from a cup of tea in a warm room, and the breath of an animal in the same room, are hardly visible, but become sensible immediately when out in the cold air, so the vapour from the gulph stream, in warm latitudes, is scarcely visible, but when it comes into the cool air from Newfoundland, it is condensed into the fogs, for which those parts are so remarkable.

The power of wind to raise water above its common level in the sea is known to us in America, by the high tides occasioned in all our seaports when a strong northeaster blows against the gulf stream.

The conclusion from these remarks is, that a vessel from Europe to North America may shorten her passage by avoiding to stem the stream, in which the thermometer will be very useful; and a vessel from America to Europe may do the same by the same means of keeping in it. It may have often happened accidentally, that voyages have been shortened by these circumstances. It is well to have command of them. . . .

With great esteem, I am, sir,
Your most obedient humble servant,

B. FRANKLIN

CHARTING THE GULF STREAM

TO

ANTHONY TODD

Craven Street, October 29, 1769.

SIR: —

DISCOURSING with Captain Folger, a very intelligent mariner of the Island of Nantucket, in New England, concerning the long passages made by some ships bound from England to New York, I received from him the following information, viz.,

That the island in which he lives is inhabited chiefly by people concerned in the whale fishery, in which they employed near 150 sail of vessels; that the whales are found generally near the edges of the *Gulph Stream*, a strong current so called, which comes out of the Gulph of Florida, passing northeasterly along the coast of America, and then turning off most easterly, running at the rate of 4, 3½, 3, and 2½ miles an hour. That the whaling business leading these people to cruise along the edges of the stream in quest of whales, they are become better acquainted with the course, breadth, strength, and extent of the same, than those navigators can well be who only cross it in their voyages to and from America, that they have opportunities of discovering the strength of it when their boats are out in the pursuit of this fish, and happen to get into the stream while the ship is out of it, or out of the stream while the ship is in it, for then they are separated very fast, and would soon loose sight of each other if care were not taken that in crossing the stream to and fro, they frequently in the same meet and speak with ships bound from England to New York, Virginia, &c. who have passages of 8, 9, and 10 weeks and are still far from land, and not likely to be in with it for some time, being engaged in that part of the stream that sets directly against them, and it is supposed that their fear of Cape Sable Shoals, George's Banks, or Nantucket Shoals, hath induced them to keep so far to the southward as unavoidable to engage them in the said Gulph Stream, which occasions the length of their voyage, since in a calm it carries them directly back, and tho' they may have fair winds, yet the current being 60 or 70 miles a day, is so much subtracted from the way they make thro' the water. At my request Captain Folger hath been so obliging as to mark for me on a chart the dimensions, course and swiftness of the Stream from its first coming out of the Gulph when it is narrowest and strongest, until it turns away to go to the southward of the Western Islands, where it is broader and weaker, and to give me withall some written directions whereby ships bound from the Banks of Newfoundland to New York may avoid the said Stream; and yet be free of danger from the banks and shoals above mentioned. As I apprehend that such chart and directions may be of use to our packets in shortning their voyages, I send them to you, that if their Lordships should think fit, so much of the chart as is contained within the red lines may be engraved, and printed, together with the remarks, at the charge of the office; or at least the manuscript copies may be made of the same for the use of the packets. The expence of the former would not much exceed the latter and would besides be of general service.

With much esteem, I am, etc.

B. FRANKLIN

Endorsed: "Craven Street, Oct 29th, 1769, Dr. Franklin to Mr. Todd. In Mr. Todd's to Mr. Pownall, of 17th Feby 1769."

DEPTH OF WATER AND SPEED *of* BOATS

TO

SIR JOHN PRINGLE

Craven Street, May 10, 1768.

SIR,

YOU may remember, that when we were travelling together in *Holland,* you remarked, that the trackschuyt in one of the stages went slower than usual, and inquired of the boatman, what might be the reason; who answered, that it had been a dry season, and the water in the canal was low. On being again asked if it was so low as that the boat touched the muddy bottom; he said, no, not so low as that, but so low as to make it harder for the horse to draw the boat. We neither of us at first could conceive that if there was water enough for the boat to swim clear of the bottom, its being deeper would make any difference; but as the man affirmed it seriously as a thing well known among them; and as the punctuality required in their stages, was likely to make such difference, if any there were, more readily observed by them, than by other watermen who did not pass so regularly and constantly backwards and forwards in the same track; I began to apprehend there might be something in it, and attempted to account for it from this consideration, that the boat in proceeding along the canal, must in every boat's length of her course, move out of her way a body of water, equal in bulk to the room her bottom took up in the water; that the water so moved, must pass on each side of her and under her bottom to get behind her; that if the passage under her bottom was straitened by the shallows, more of that water must pass by her sides, and with a swifter motion, which would retard her, as moving the contrary way; or that the water becoming lower behind the boat than before, she was pressed back by the weight of its difference in height, and her motion retarded by having that weight constantly to overcome. But as it is often lost time to attempt accounting for uncertain facts, I determined to make an experiment of this, when I should have convenient time and opportunity.

After our return to *England,* as often as I happened to be on the *Thames,* I inquired of our watermen whether they were sensible of any difference in rowing over shallow or deep water. I found them all agreeing in the fact, that there was a very great difference, but they differed widely in expressing the quantity of the difference; some supposing it was equal to a mile in six, others to a mile in three, &c. As I did not recollect to have met with any mention of this matter in our philosophical books, and conceiving that if the difference should really be great, it might be an object of consideration in the many projects now on foot for digging new navigable canals in this island, I lately put my design of making the experiment in execution, in the following manner.

I provided a trough of plained boards fourteen feet long, six inches wide and six inches deep, in the clear, filled with water within half an inch of the edge, to represent a canal. I had a loose board of nearly the same length and breadth, that being put into the water might be sunk to any depth, and fixed by little wedges where I would chuse to have it stay in order to make different depths of water, leaving the surface at the same height with regard to the sides of the trough. I had a little boat in form of a lighter or boat of burthen, six inches long, two inches and a quarter wide, and one inch and a quarter deep. When swimming, it drew one inch water. To give motion to the boat, I fixed one end of a long silk thread to its bow, just even with the water's edge, the other end passed over a well made brass pully, of about an inch diameter, turning freely on a small axis; and a shilling was the weight. Then placing the boat at one end of the trough, the weight would draw it through the water to the other.

Not having a watch that shows seconds, in order to measure the time taken up by the boat in passing from end to end, I counted as fast as I could count to ten repeatedly, keeping an account of the number of tens on my fingers. And as much as possible to correct any little inequalities in my counting, I repeated the experiment a number of times at each depth of water, that I might take the medium. And the following are the results.

Water 1½ inches deep.	2 inches.	4½ inches.
1st exp. 100	94	79
2 104	93	78
3 104	91	77
4 106	87	79
5 100	88	79
6 99	86	80
7 100	90	79
8 100	88	81
813	717	642
Medium 101	Medium 89	Medium 79

I made many other experiments, but the above are those in which I was most exact; and they serve sufficiently to show that the difference is considerable. Between the deepest and shallowest it appears to be somewhat more than one fifth. So that supposing large canals and boats and depths of water to bear the same proportions, and that four men or horses would draw a boat in deep water four leagues in four hours, it would require five to draw the same boat in the same time as far in shallow water; or four would require five hours.

Whether this difference is of consequence enough to justify a greater expence in deepening canals, is a matter of calculation, which our ingenious engineers in that way will readily determine.

I am, &c.
B. FRANKLIN.

DISTILLATION OF SALT WATER

TO

MISS MARY STEVENSON

Craven Street, Aug. 10, 1761.

DEAR POLLEY

. . . .

IN yours of May 19, which I have before me, you speak of the ease with which salt water may be made fresh by distillation, supposing it to be, as I had said, that in evaporation the air would take up water, but not the salt that was mix'd with it. It is true, that distill'd sea water will not be salt, but there are other disagreable qualities that rise with the water in distillation; which indeed several besides Dr. Hales have endeavoured by sundry means to prevent; but as yet their methods have not been brought much into use. . . .

I have a singular opinion on this subject, which I will venture to communicate to you, tho' I doubt you will rank it among my whims. It is certain that the skin has *imbibing* as well as *discharging* pores; witness the effects of a blister plaister, &c. I have read, that a man, hired by a physician to stand by way of experiment in the open air naked during a moist night, weighed near 3 pounds heavier in the morning. I have often observed myself, that, however thirsty I may have been before going into the water to swim, I am never long so in the water. These imbibing pores, however, are very fine, perhaps fine enough in filtring to separate salt from water; for, tho' I have soak'd by swimming, when a boy, several hours in the day for several days successively in salt water, I never found my blood and juices salted by that means, so as to make me thirsty or feel a salt taste in my mouth: And it is remarkable, that the flesh of sea fish, tho' bred in salt water, is not salt.

Hence I imagine, that, if people at sea, distress'd by thirst when their fresh water is unfortunately spent, would make bathing-tubs of their empty water casks, and, filling them with sea water, sit in them an hour or two each day, they might be greatly reliev'd. Perhaps keeping their clothes constantly wet might have an almost equal effect; and this without danger of catching cold. Men do not catch cold by wet clothes at sea. Damp, but not wet linen may possibly give colds; but no one catches cold by bathing, and no clothes can be wetter than water itself. Why damp clothes should then occasion colds, is a curious question, the discussion of which I reserve for a future letter, or some future conversation.

Adieu, my dear little philosopher. Present my respectful compliments to the good ladies, your aunts, and to Miss Pitt; and believe me ever

Your affectionate Friend,
And humble Servant,

B. FRANKLIN.

BEHAVIOR OF OIL
ON WATER

TO

JOHN PRINGLE

Philadelphia, Dec. 1, 1762.

SIR,

DURING our passage to Madeira, the weather being warm, and the cabbin windows constantly open for the benefit of the air, the candles at night flared and run very much, which was an inconvenience. At Madeira we got oil to burn, and with a common glass tumbler or beaker, slung in wire, and suspended to the cieling of the cabbin, and a little wire hoop for the wick, furnish'd with corks to float on the oil, I made an Italian lamp, that gave us very good light all over the table. That glass at bottom contained water to about one third of its height; another third was taken up with oil; the rest was left empty that the sides of the glass might protect the flame from the wind. There is nothing remarkable in all this; but what follows is particular. At supper, looking on the lamp, I remarked that tho' the surface of the oil was perfectly tranquil, and duly preserved its position and distance with regard to the brim of the glass, the water under the oil was in great commotion, rising and falling in irregular waves, which continued during the whole evening. The lamp was kept burning as a watch-light all night, till the oil was spent, and the water only remain'd. In the morning I observed, that though the motion of the ship continued the same the water was now quiet, and its surface as tranquil as that of the oil had been the evening before. At night again, when oil was put upon it, the water resum'd its irregular motions, rising in high waves almost to the surface of the oil, but without disturbing the smooth level of that surface. And this was repeated every day during the voyage.

Since my arrival in America, I have repeated the experiment frequently thus. I have put a pack-thread round a tumbler, with strings of the same, from each side, meeting above it in a knot at about a foot distance from the top of the tumbler. Then putting in as much water as would fill about one third part of the tumbler, I lifted it up by the knot, and swung it to and fro in the air; when the water appeared to keep its place in the tumbler as steadily as if it had been ice. But pouring gently in upon the water about as much oil, and then again swinging it in the air as before, the tranquility before possessed by the water was transferred to the surface of the oil, and the water under it was agitated with the same commotions as at sea.

I have shewn this experiment to a number of ingenious persons. Those who are but slightly acquainted with the principles of hydrostatics, &c. are apt to fancy immediately that they understand it, and readily attempt to explain it; but their explanations have been different, and to me not very intelligible. Others more deeply skilled in those principles, seem to wonder at it, and promise to consider it. And I think it is worth considering; for a new appearance, and if it cannot be explained by our old principles, may afford us new ones, of use perhaps in explaining some other obscure parts of natural knowledge. *I am, &c.*

B. FRANKLIN.

EARLIEST ACCOUNT
of MARSH GAS

TO

JOSEPH PRIESTLEY

Craven Street, April 10, 1774.

DEAR SIR,

IN compliance with your request, I have endeavoured to recollect the circumstances of the American experiments I formerly mentioned to you, of raising a flame on the surface of some waters there.

When I passed through New Jersey in 1764, I heard it several times mentioned, that, by applying a lighted candle near the surface of some of their rivers, a sudden flame would catch and spread on the water, continuing to burn for near half a minute. But the accounts I received were so imperfect, that I could form no guess at the cause of such an effect, and rather doubted the truth of it. I had no opportunity of seeing the experiment; but, calling to see a friend who happened to be just returning home from making it himself, I learned from him the manner of it; which was to choose a shallow place, where the bottom could be reached by a walking-stick, and was muddy; the mud was first to be stirred with the stick, and, when a number of small bubbles began to arise from it, the candle was applied. The flame was so sudden and so strong, that it catched his ruffle and spoiled it, as I saw. New Jersey having many pine-trees in many parts of it, I then imagined that something like a volatile oil of turpentine might be mixed with the waters from a pine-swamp, but this supposition did not quite satisfy me. I mentioned the fact to some philosophical friends on my return to England, but it was not much attended to. I suppose I was thought a little too credulous.

In 1765, the Reverend Dr. Chandler received a letter from Dr. Finley, President of the College in that province, relating the same experiment. It was read at the Royal Society, November 21st of that year, but not printed in the Transactions; perhaps because it was thought too strange to be true, and some ridicule might be apprehended, if any member should attempt to repeat it, in order to ascertain, or refute it. The following is a copy of that account.

"A worthy gentleman, who lives at a few miles distance, informed me, that in a certain small cove of a mill-pond, near his house, he was surprised to see the surface of the water blaze like inflamed spirits. I soon after went to the place, and made the experiment with the same success. The bottom of the creek was muddy, and when stirred up, so as to cause a considerable curl on the surface, and a lighted candle held within two or three inches of it, the whole surface was in a blaze, as instantly as the vapour of warm inflammable spirits, and continued, when strongly agitated, for the space of several seconds. It was at first imagined to be peculiar to that place; but upon trial it was soon found, that such a bottom in other places exhibited the same phenomenon. The discovery was accidentally made by one belonging to the mill."

I have tried the experiment twice here in England, but without success. The first was in a slow running water with a muddy bottom. The second in a stagnant water at the bottom of a deep ditch. Being some time employed in stirring this water, I ascribed an intermitting fever, which seized me a few days after, to my breathing too much of that foul air, which I stirred up from the bottom, and which I could not avoid while I stooped, endeavouring to kindle it. The discoveries you have lately made, of the manner in which inflammable air is in some cases produced, may throw light on this experiment, and explain its succeeding in some cases, and not in others.

With the highest esteem, and respect
I am, dear Sir, your most obedient humble servant,

B. FRANKLIN.

SMALLPOX AND CANCER

TO

MRS. JANE MECOM

Philadelphia, June 19, 1731.

DEAR SISTER,

. . . .

WE have had the smallpox here lately, which raged violently while it lasted. There have been about fifty persons inoculated, who all recovered except a child of the doctor's upon whom the smallpox appeared within a day or two after the operation, and who is therefore thought to have been certainly infected before. In one family in my neighbourhood there appeared a great mortality. Mr. George Claypoole . . . had, by industry, acquired a great estate, and being in excellent business, a merchant, would probably have doubled it, had he lived according to the common course of years. He died first, suddenly; within a short time died his best negro; then one of his children; then a negro woman; then two children more, buried at the same time; then two more; so that I saw two double buryings come out of the house in one week. None were left in the family, but the mother and one child, and both their lives till lately despaired of; so that all the father's wealth, which everybody thought, a little while ago, had heirs enough, and no one would have given sixpence for the reversion, was in a few weeks brought to the greatest probability of being divided among strangers; so uncertain are all human affairs. The dissolution of this family is generally ascribed to an imprudent use of quicksilver in the cure of the itch, Mr. Claypoole applying it as he thought proper, without consulting a physician for fear of charges; and the smallpox coming upon them at the same time made their case desperate.

But what gives me the greatest concern, is the account you give me of my sister Holmes's [Mary Franklin Holmes] misfortune. I know a cancer in the breast is often thought incurable; yet we have here in town a kind of shell made of some wood, cut at a proper time, by some man of great skill, (as they say,) which has done wonders in that disease among us, being worn for some time on the breast. I am not apt to be superstitiously fond of believing such things, but the instances are so well attested, as sufficiently to convince the most incredulous.

This, if I have interest enough to procure, as I think I have, I will borrow for a time, and send it to you, and hope the doctors you have will at least allow the experiment to be tried, and shall rejoice to hear it has the accustomed effect.

.   .   .   .

B. FRANKLIN.

RESTORATION *of* LIFE *by* SUN RAYS

TO

BARBEU DUBOURG

[1773]

YOUR observations on the causes of death, and the experiments which you propose for recalling to life those who appear to be killed by lightning, demonstrate equally your sagacity and your humanity. It appears that the doctrines of life and death in general are yet but little understood.

A toad buried in sand will live, it is said, till the sand becomes petrified; and then, being enclosed in the stone, it may still live for we know not how many ages. The facts which are cited in support of this opinion are too numerous, and too circumstantial, not to deserve a certain degree of credit. As we are accustomed to see all the animals with which we are acquainted eat and drink, it appears to us difficult to conceive how a toad can be supported in such a dungeon; but if we reflect that the necessity of nourishment which animals experience in their ordinary state proceeds from the continual waste of their substance by perspiration, it will appear less incredible that some animals in a torpid state, perspiring less because they use no exercise, should have less need of aliment; and that others, which are covered with scales or shells, which stop perspiration, such as land and sea turtles, serpents, and some species of fish, should be able to subsist a considerable time without any nourishment whatever. A plant, with its flowers, fades and dies immediately, if exposed to the air without having its root immersed in a humid soil, from which it may draw a sufficient quantity of moisture to supply that which exhales from its substance and is carried off continually by the air. Perhaps, however, if it were buried in quicksilver, it might preserve for a considerable space of time its vegetable life, its smell, and colour. If this be the case, it might prove a commodious method of transporting from distant countries those delicate plants, which are unable to sustain the inclemency of the weather at sea, and which require particular care and attention. I have seen an instance of common flies preserved in a manner somewhat similar. They had been drowned in Madeira wine, apparently about the time when it was bottled in Virginia, to be sent hither (to London). At the opening of one of the bottles, at the house of a friend where I then was, three drowned flies fell into the first glass that was filled. Having heard it remarked that drowned flies were capable of being revived by the rays of the sun, I proposed making the experiment upon these; they were therefore exposed to the sun upon a sieve, which had been employed to strain them out of the wine. In less than three hours, two of them began by degrees to recover life. They commenced by some convulsive motions of the thighs, and at length they raised themselves upon their legs, wiped their eyes with their fore feet, beat and brushed their wings with their hind feet, and soon after began to fly, finding themselves in Old England, without knowing how they came thither. The third continued lifeless till sunset, when, losing all hopes of him, he was thrown away.

I wish it were possible, from this instance, to invent a method of embalming drowned persons, in such a manner that they may be recalled to life at any period, however distant; for having a very ardent desire to see and observe the state of America a hundred years hence, I should prefer to any ordinary death the being immersed in a cask of Madeira wine, with a few friends, till that time, to be then recalled to life by the solar warmth of my dear country! But since in all probability we live in an age too early and too near the infancy of science, to hope to see such an art brought in our time to its perfection, I must for the present content myself with the treat, which you are so kind as to promise me, of the resurrection of a fowl or a turkey cock.

I am, &c.

B. FRANKLIN.

SCIENTIFIC DEDUCTIONS
and CONJECTURES

CAUSE OF COLDS

TO

BENJAMIN RUSH

London, July 14, 1773.

DEAR SIR,

. . . .

I SHALL communicate your judicious remark, relating to the septic quality of the air transpired by patients in putrid diseases, to my friend Dr. Priestley. I hope that after having discovered the benefit of fresh and cool air applied to the sick, people will begin to suspect that possibly it may do no harm to the well. I have not seen Dr. Cullen's book, but am glad to hear that he speaks of catarrhs or colds by contagion. I have long been satisfied from observation, that besides the general colds now termed *influenzas,* (which may possibly spread by contagion, as well as by a particular quality of the air), people often catch cold from one another when shut up together in close rooms, coaches, &c., and when sitting near and conversing so as to breathe in each other's transpiration; the disorder being in a certain state. I think, too, that it is the frouzy, corrupt air from animal substances, and the perspired matter from our bodies, which being long confined in beds not lately used, and clothes not lately worn, and books long shut up in close rooms, obtains that kind of putridity, which occasions the colds observed upon sleeping in, wearing, and turning over such bed-clothes, or books, and not their coldness or dampness. From these causes, but more from too full living, with too little exercise, proceed in my opinion most of the disorders, which for about one hundred and fifty years past the English have called *colds.*

As to Dr. Cullen's cold or catarrh *a frigore,* I question whether such an one ever existed. Travelling in our severe winters, I have suffered cold sometimes to an extremity only short of freezing, but this did not make me *catch cold.* And, for moisture, I have been in the river every evening two or three hours for a fortnight together, when one would suppose I might imbibe enough of it to *take cold* if humidity could give it; but no such effect ever followed. Boys never get cold by swimming. Nor are people at sea, or who live at Bermudas, or St. Helena, small islands, where the air must be ever moist from the dashing and breaking of waves against their rocks on all sides, more subject to colds than those who inhabit part of a continent where the air is driest. Dampness may indeed assist in producing putridity and those miasmata which infect us with the disorder we call a cold; but of itself can never by a little addition of moisture hurt a body filled with watery fluids from head to foot.

With great esteem, and sincere wishes for your welfare, I am, Sir,

Your most obedient humble servant,

B. FRANKLIN.

DEFINITION *of* *a* COLD

IT is a siziness and thickness of the blood, whereby the smaller vessels are obstructed, and the perspirable matter retained, which being retained offends both by its quantity and quality; by quantity, as it overfills the vessels, and by its quality, as part of it is acrid, and being retained, produces coughs and sneezing by irritation.

HEAT AND COLD

TO

JOHN LINING

at Charleston, South Carolina

New York, April 14, 1757.

SIR,

· · · · · · · · · · ·

PROFESSOR SIMSON, of Glasgow, lately communicated to me some curious experiments of a physician of his acquaintance, by which it appeared that an extraordinary degree of cold, even to freezing, might be produced by evaporation. I have not had leisure to repeat and examine more than the first and easiest of them, viz. Wet the ball of a thermometer by a feather dipped in spirit of wine, which has been kept in the same room, and has, of course, the same degree of heat or cold. The mercury sinks presently three or four degrees, and the quicker, if, during the evaporation, you blow on the ball with bellows; a second wetting and blowing, when the mercury is down, carries it yet lower. I think I did not get it lower than five or six degrees from where it naturally stood, which was, at that time, sixty. But it is said, that a vessel of water being placed in another somewhat larger, containing spirit, in such a manner that the vessel of water is surrounded with the spirit, and both placed under the receiver of an air-pump; on exhausting the air, the spirit, evaporating, leaves such a degree of cold as to freeze the water, though the thermometer, in the open air, stands many degrees above the freezing point.

I know not how this phenomenon is to be accounted for; but it gives me occasion to mention some loose notions relating to heat and cold, which I have for some time entertained, but not yet reduced into any form. Allowing common fire, as well as electrical, to be a fluid capable of permeating other bodies, and seeking an equilibrium, I imagine some bodies are better fitted by nature to be conductors of that fluid than others; and that, generally, those which are the best conductors of the electrical fluid, are also the best conductors of this; and *e contra.*

Thus a body which is a good conductor of fire readily receives it into its substance, and conducts it through the whole to all the parts, as metals and water do; and if two bodies, both good conductors, one heated, the other in its common state, are brought into contact with each other, the body which has most fire readily communicates of it to that which had least, and that which had least readily receives it, till an equilibrium is produced. Thus, if you take a dollar between your fingers with one hand, and a piece of wood, of the same dimensions, with the other, and bring both at the same time to the flame of a candle, you will find yourself obliged to drop the dollar before you drop the wood, because it conducts the heat of the candle sooner to your flesh. Thus, if a silver tea-pot had a handle of the same metal, it would conduct the heat from the water to the hand, and become too hot to be used; we therefore give to a metal tea-pot a handle of wood, which is not so good a conductor as metal. But a china or stone tea-pot being in some degree of the nature of glass, which is not a good conductor of heat, may have a handle of the same stuff. Thus, also, a damp moist air shall make a man more sensible of cold, or chill him more, than a dry air that is colder, because a moist air is fitter to receive and conduct away the heat of his body. This fluid, entering bodies in great quantity first expands them by separating their parts a little, afterwards, by farther separating their parts, it renders solids fluid, and at length dissipates their parts in air. Take this fluid from melted lead, or from water, the parts cohere again; (the first grows solid, the latter becomes ice;) and this is sooner done by the means of good conductors. Thus, if you take, as I have done, a square bar of lead, four inches long, and one inch thick, together with three pieces of wood planed to the same dimensions, and lay them, as in the margin, on a smooth board, fixed so as not to be easily separated or moved, and pour into

the cavity they form, as much melted lead as will fill it, you will see the melted lead chill, and become firm, on the side next the leaden bar, some time before it chills on the other three sides in contact with the wooden bars, though, before the lead was poured in, they might all be supposed to have the same degree of heat or coldness, as they had been exposed in the same room to the same air. You will likewise observe, that the leaden bar, as it has cooled the melted lead more than the wooden bars have done, so it is itself more heated by the melted lead. There is a certain quantity of this fluid, called fire, in every living human body, which fluid, being in due proportion, keeps the parts of the flesh and blood at such a just distance from each other, as that the flesh and nerves are supple, and the blood fit for circulation. If part of this due proportion of fire be conducted away, by means of a contact with other bodies, as air, water, or metals, the parts of our skin and flesh that come into such contact first draw more near together than is agreeable, and give that sensation which we call cold; and if too much be conveyed away, the body stiffens, the blood ceases to flow, and death ensues. On the other hand, if too much of this fluid be communicated to the flesh, the parts are separated too far, and pain ensues, as when they are separated by a pin or lancet. The sensation, that the separation by fire occasions, we call heat, or burning. My desk on which I now write, and the lock of my desk, are both exposed to the same temperature of the air, and have therefore the same degree of heat or cold; yet if I lay my hand successively on the wood and on the metal, the latter feels much the coldest, not that it is really so, but, being a better conductor, it more readily than the wood takes away and draws into itself the fire that was in my skin. Accordingly if I lay one hand, part on the lock, and part on the wood, and, after it has lain so some time, I feel both parts with my other hand, I find that part that has been in contact with the lock, very sensibly colder to the touch, than the part that lay on the wood. How a living animal obtains its quantity of this fluid, called fire, is a curious question. I have shewn, that some bodies (as metals) have a power of attracting it stronger than others; and I have sometimes suspected, that a living body had some power of attracting out of the air, or other bodies, the heat it wanted. Thus metals hammered, or repeatedly bent grow hot in the bent or hammer'd part. But when I consider that air, in contact with the body, cools it; that the surrounding air is rather heated by its contact with the body; that every breath of cooler air, drawn in, carries off part of the body's heat when it passes out again; that therefore there must be some fund in the body for producing it, or otherwise the animal would soon grow cold; I have been rather inclined to think, that the fluid *fire*, as well as the fluid *air*, is attracted by plants in their growth, and becomes consolidated with the other materials of which they are formed, and makes a great part of their substance. That, when they come to be digested, and to suffer in the vessels a kind of fermentation, part of the fire, as well as part of the air, recovers its fluid, active state again, and diffuses itself in the body digesting and separating it. That the fire, so reproduced by digestion and separation, continually leaving the body, its place is supplied by fresh quantities, arising from the continual separation. That whatever quickens the motion of the fluids in an animal quickens the separation, and reproduces more of the fire, as exercise. That all the fire emitted by wood and other combustibles when burning existed in them before in a solid state, being only discover'd when separating. That some fossils, as sulphur, sea-coal, &c., contain a great deal of solid fire. And that in short, what escapes and is dissipated in the burning of bodies, besides water and earth, is generally the air and fire that before made parts of the solid. Thus I imagine, that animal heat arises by or from a kind of fermentation in the juices of the body, in the same manner as heat arises in the liquors preparing for distillation, wherein there is a separation of the spirituous, from the watery and earthy parts. And it is remarkable, that the liquor in a distiller's vat, when in its highest and best state of fermentation, as I have been inform'd, has the same degree of heat with the human body, that is about 94 or 96.

Thus, as by a constant supply of fuel in a chimney, you keep a warm room, so, by a constant supply of food in the stomach, you keep a warm body; only where little exercise is used, the heat may possibly be conducted away too fast; in which case such materials are to be used for cloathing and bedding, against the effects of an immediate contact of the air, as are, in themselves, bad conductors of heat, and, consequently prevent its being communicated thro' their substances to the air. Hence what is called *warmth* in wool, and its preference, on that account, to linnen; wool not being so good a conductor. And hence all the natural coverings of animals, to keep them warm, are such as retain and confine the natural heat in the body by being bad conductors, such as wool, hair, feathers, and the silk by which the silk-worm, in its tender embrio state, is first cloathed. Cloathing thus considered does not make a man warm by *giving* warmth, but by *preventing* the too quick dissipation of the heat produced in his body, and so occasioning an accumulation.

There is another curious question I will just venture to touch upon, viz. Whence arises the sudden extraordinary degree of cold, perceptible on mixing some chymical liquors, and even on mixing salt and snow, where the composition appears colder than the coldest of the ingredients? I have never seen the chymical mixtures made; but salt and snow I have often mixed myself, and am fully satisfied that the composition feels much colder to the touch, and lowers the mercury in the thermometer more, than either ingredient would do separately. I suppose, with others, that cold is nothing more than the absence of heat or fire. Now if the quantity of fire before contained or diffused in the snow and salt was expell'd in the uniting of the two matters, it must be driven away either thro' the air or the vessel containing them. If it is driven off thro' the air, it must warm the air; and a thermometer held over the mixture, without touching it, would discover the heat, by the rising of the mercury, as it must, and always does, in warmer air.

This indeed I have not try'd but I should guess it would rather be driven off thro' the vessel, especially if the vessel be metal, as being a better conductor than air, and so one should find the bason warmer after such mixture. But on the contrary the vessel grows cold, and even water, in which the vessel is sometimes placed for the experiment, freezes into hard ice on the bason. Now I know not how to account for this, otherwise than by supposing, that the composition is a better conductor of fire than the ingredients separately and like the lock compar'd with the wood, has a stronger power of attracting fire, and does accordingly attract it suddenly from the fingers, or a thermometer put into it, from the bason that contains it, and from the water in contact with the outside of the bason; so that the fingers have the sensation of extreme cold, by being depriv'd of much of their natural fire; the thermometer sinks, by having part of its fire drawn out of the mercury; the bason grows colder to the touch, as by having its fire drawn into the mixture, it is become more capable of drawing and receiving it from the hand, and thro' the bason, the water loses its fire that kept it fluid; so it becomes ice. One would expect, that from all this attracted acquisition of fire to the composition, it should become warmer; and, in fact, the snow and salt dissolve at the same time into water without freezing.

. . . .

Your etc

B. FRANKLIN

COLD BY EVAPORATION

JOHN LINING

at Charleston

London, June 17, 1758.

DEAR SIR,

IN a former letter I mentioned the experiment for cooling bodies by evaporation, and that I had, by repeatedly wetting the thermometer with common spirits, brought the mercury down five or six degrees. Being lately at *Cambridge,* and mentioning this in conversation with Dr. *Hadley,* professor of chemistry there, he proposed repeating the experiments with ether, instead of common spirits, as the ether is much quicker in evaporation. We accordingly went to his chamber, where he had both ether and a thermometer. By dipping first the ball of the thermometer into the ether, it appeared that the ether was precisely of the same temperament with the thermometer, which stood then at 65; for it made no alteration in the height of the little column of mercury. But when the thermometer was taken out of the ether, and the ether, with which the ball was wet, began to evaporate, the mercury sunk several degrees. The wetting was then repeated by a feather that had been dipped into the ether, when the mercury sunk still lower.

We continued this operation, one of us wetting the ball, and another of the company blowing on it with the bellows, to quicken the evaporation, the mercury sinking all the time, till it came down to 7, which is 25 degrees below the freezing point, when we left off. Soon after it passed the freezing point, a thin coat of ice began to cover the ball. Whether this was water collected and condensed by the coldness of the ball, from the moisture in the air, or from our breath; or whether the feather when dipped into the ether, might not sometimes go through it, and bring up some of the water that was under it, I am not certain; perhaps all might contribute. The ice continued increasing till we ended the experiment, when it appeared near a quarter of an inch thick all over the ball, with a number of small *spicula*, pointing outwards. From this experiment one may see the possibility of freezing a man to death on a warm summer's day, if he were to stand in a passage through which the wind blew briskly, and to be wet frequently with ether, a spirit that is more inflammable than brandy, or common spirits of wine.

It is but within these few years, that the *European* philosophers seem to have known this power in nature, of cooling bodies by evaporation. But in the east they have long been acquainted with it. A friend tells me, there is a passage in *Bernier's* Travels through *Indostan*, written near one hundred years ago, that mentions it as a practice (in travelling over dry desarts in that hot climate) to carry water in flasks wrapt in wet woollen cloths, and hung on the shady side of the camel, or carriage, but in the free air; whereby, as the cloths gradually grow drier, the water contained in the flasks is made cool. They have likewise a kind of earthen pots, unglaz'd, which let the water gradually and slowly ooze through their pores, so as to keep the outside a little wet, notwithstanding the continual evaporation, which gives great coldness to the vessel, and the water contained in it. Even our common sailors seem to have had some notion of this property; for I remember, that being at sea, when I was a youth, I observed one of the sailors, during a calm in the night, often wetting his finger in his mouth, and then holding it up in the air, to discover, as he said, if the air had any motion, and from which side it came; and this he expected to do, by finding one side of his finger grow suddenly cold, and from that side he should look for the next wind; which I then laughed at as a fancy.

May not several phænomena, hitherto unconsidered, or unaccounted for, be explained by this property? During the hot *Sunday* at *Philadelphia,* in *June* 1750, when the thermometer was up at 100 in the shade, I sat in my chamber without exercise, only reading or writing, with no other cloaths on than a shirt, and a pair of long linen drawers, the windows all open, and a brisk wind blowing through the house; the sweat ran off the backs of my hands, and my shirt was often so wet, as to induce me to call for dry ones to put on. In this situation, one might have expected, that the natural heat of the body 96, added to the heat of the air 100, should jointly have created or produced a much greater degree of heat in the body; but the fact was, that my body never grew so hot as the air that surrounded it, or the inanimate bodies immersed in the same air. For I remember well, that the desk, when I laid my arm upon it; a chair, when I sat down upon it; and a dry shirt out of the drawer, when I put it on, all felt exceedingly warm to me, as if they had been warmed before a fire. And I suppose a dead body would have acquired the temperature of the air, though a living one, by continual sweating, and by the evaporation of that sweat, was kept cold.

[167]

May not this be a reason why our reapers in *Pensylvania*, working in the open field in the clear hot sunshine common in our harvest-time, find themselves well able to go through that labour, without being much incommoded by the heat, while they continue to sweat, and while they supply matter for keeping up that sweat, by drinking frequently of a thin evaporable liquor, water mixed with rum; but, if the sweat stops, they drop, and sometimes die suddenly, if a sweating is not again brought on by drinking that liquor, or, as some rather chuse in that case, a kind of hot punch, made with water, mixed with honey, and a considerable proportion of vinegar? May there not be in negroes a quicker evaporation of the perspirable matter from their skins and lungs, which, by cooling them more, enables them to bear the sun's heat better than whites do? (if that is a fact, as it is said to be; for the alledg'd necessity of having negroes rather than whites, to work in the *West India* fields, is founded upon it) though the colour of their skins would otherwise make them more sensible of the sun's heat, since black cloth heats much sooner, and more, in the sun, than white cloth. I am persuaded, from several instances happening within my knowledge, that they do not bear cold weather so well as the whites; they will perish when exposed to a less degree of it, and are more apt to have their limbs frost-bitten; and may not this be from the same cause?

Would not the earth grow much hotter under the summer sun, if a constant evaporation from its surface, greater as the sun shines stronger, did not, by tending to cool it, balance, in some degree, the warmer effects of the sun's rays? Is it not owing to the constant evaporation from the surface of every leaf, that trees, though shone on by the sun, are always, even the leaves themselves, cool to our sense? at least, much cooler than they would otherwise be? May it not be owing to this, that fanning ourselves when warm, does really cool us, though the air is itself warm that we drive with the fan upon our faces? For the atmosphere round, and next to our bodies, having imbibed as much of the perspired vapour as it can well contain, receives no more, and the evaporation is therefore check'd, and retarded, till we drive away that atmosphere, and bring dryer air in its place, that will receive the vapour, and thereby facilitate and increase the evaporation? Certain it is, that mere blowing of air on a dry body does not cool it, as any one may satisfy himself, by blowing with a bellows on the dry ball of a thermometer; the mercury will not fall; if it moves at all, it rather rises, as being warmed by the friction of the air on its surface.

To these queries of imagination, I will only add one practical observation; that wherever it is thought proper to give ease, in cases of painful inflammation in the flesh (as from burnings, or the like), by cooling the part; linen cloths wet with spirit, and applied to the part inflamed, will produce the coolness required, better than if wet with water, and will continue it longer. For water, though cold when first applied, will soon acquire warmth from the flesh, as it does not evaporate fast enough; but the cloths wet with spirit, will continue cold as long as any spirit is left to keep up the evaporation, the parts warmed escaping as soon as they are warmed, and carrying off the heat with them.

I am, Sir, &c.
B.F[RANKLIN]

ON SPRINGS

TO

JARED ELIOT

Philadelphia, July 16, 1747

DEAR SIR,

. . . .

I THANK you for the curious facts you have communicated to me relating to springs. I think with you, that most springs arise from rains, dews, or ponds, on higher grounds; yet possibly some, that break out near the tops of high hollow mountains, may proceed from the abyss, or from water in the caverns of the earth, rarefied by its internal heat, and raised in vapour, till the cold region near the tops of such mountains condenses the vapour into water again, which comes forth in springs, and runs down on the outside of the mountains, as it ascended on the inside. There it is said to be a large spring near the top of Teneriffe; and that mountain was formerly a volcano, consequently hollow within. Such springs, if such there be, may properly be called springs of *distill'd* water.

Now I mention mountains, it occurs to tell you, that the great Apalachian mountains, which run from York River back of these colonies, to the Bay of Mexico, show in many places, near the highest parts of them, strata of sea shells; in some places the marks of them are in the solid rocks. It is certainly the *Wreck* of a world we live on! We have specimens of these sea shell rocks, broken off near the tops of these mountains, brought and deposited in our Library as curiosities. If you have not seen the like, I'll send you a piece. Farther, about mountains (for ideas will string themselves like ropes of onions); when I was once riding in your country, Mr. Walker show'd me at a distance the bluff side or end of a mountain, which appeared striped from top to bottom, and told me the stone or rock of that mountain was divided by nature into pillars; of this I should be glad to have a particular account from you. I think I was somewhere near New Haven when I saw it.

. . . .

B. FRANKLIN.

TIDES AND RIVERS

TO

MISS MARY STEVENSON

London, Sept. 13, 1760

MY DEAR FRIEND,

I HAVE your agreable letter from Bristol, which I take this first leisure hour to answer, having for some time been much engag'd in business.

Your first question, *What is the reason the water at this place, tho' cold at the spring, becomes warm by pumping?* it will be most prudent in me to forbear attempting to answer, till, by a more circumstantial account, you assure me of the fact. I own I should expect that operation to warm, not so much the water pump'd, as the person pumping. The rubbing of dry solids together has been long observ'd to produce heat; but the like effect has never yet, that I have heard, been produc'd by the mere agitation of fluids, or friction of fluids with solids. Water in a bottle, shook for hours by a mill-hopper, it is said, discover'd no sensible addition of heat. The production of animal heat by exercise is therefore to be accounted for in another manner, which I may hereafter endeavour to make you acquainted with.

This prudence of not attempting to give reasons before one is sure of facts, I learned from one of your sex, who, as Selden tells us, being in company with some gentlemen that were viewing and considering something which they call'd a Chinese Shoe, and disputing earnestly about the manner of wearing it, and how it could possibly be put on; put in her word, and said modestly, *Gentlemen, are you sure it is a shoe? Should not that be settled first?*

But I shall now endeavour to explain what I said to you about the tide in rivers, and to that end shall make a figure, which, tho' not very like a river, may serve to convey my meaning. Suppose a canal 140 miles long, communicating at one end with the sea, and fill'd therefore with sea water. I chuse a canal at first, rather than a river, to throw out of consideration the effects produced by the streams of fresh water from the land, the inequality in breadth, and the crookedness of courses.

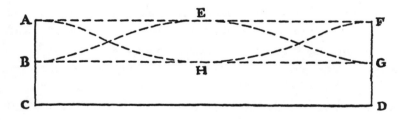

Let A,C, be the head of the canal; C,D, the bottom of it; D,F, the open mouth of it, next the sea. Let the strait prick'd line, B,G, represent low-water mark, the whole length of the canal. A,F, high-water mark: Now if a person, standing at E, and observing, at the time of high water there, that the canal is quite full at that place up to the line E, should conclude that the canal is equally full to the same height from end to end, and therefore there was as much more water come into the canal since it was down at low-water mark, as would be included in the oblong space A,B,G,F, he would be greatly mistaken. For the tide is *a wave,* and the top of the wave, which makes high water, as well as every other lower part, is progressive; and it is high water successively, but not at the same time, in all the several points between G,F, and A,B. And in such a length as I have mention'd, it is low water at F,G, and also at A,B, at or near the same time with its being high water at E; so that the surface of the water in the canal, during that situation, is properly represented by the curve prick'd line, B,E,G. And on the other hand, when it is low water at E,H, it is high water both at F,G, and at A,B, at or near the same time; and the surface would then be describ'd by the inverted curve line, A,H,F.

In this view of the case, you will easily see that there must be very little more water in the canal at what we call high water, than there is at low water, those terms not relating to the whole canal at the same time, but successively to its parts. And, if you suppose the canal six times as long, the case would not vary as to the quantity of water at different times of the tide; there would only be six waves in the canal at the same time, instead of one, and the hollows in the water would be equal to the hills.

That this is not mere theory, but conformable to fact, we know by our long rivers in America. The Delaware, on which Philadelphia stands, is in this particular similar to the canal I have supposed of one wave; for when it is high water at the capes or mouth of the river, it is also high water at Philadelphia, which stands about 140 miles from the sea; and there is at the same time a low water in the middle between the two high waters; where, when it comes to be high water, it is at the same time low water at the capes and at Philadelphia. And the longer rivers have some a wave and half, some two, three, or four waves, according to their length. In the shorter rivers of this island, one may see the same thing in part; for instance, it is high water at Gravesend an hour before it is highwater at London Bridge; and 20 miles below Gravesend an hour before it is high water at Gravesend. Therefore at the time of high water at Gravesend the top of the wave is there, and the water is then not so high by some feet where the top of the wave was an hour before, or where it will be an hour after, as it is just then at Gravesend.

Now we are not to suppose that because the swell or top of the wave runs at the rate of 20 miles an hour, that therefore the current, or water itself of which the wave is compos'd, runs at that rate. Far from it. To conceive this motion of a wave, make a small experiment or two. Fasten one end of a cord in a window near the top of a house, and let the other end come down to the ground; take this end in your hand, and you may, by a sudden motion, occasion a wave in the cord that will run quite up to the window; but tho' the wave is progressive from your hand to the window, the parts of the rope do not proceed with the wave, but remain where they were, except only that kind of motion that produces the wave. So if you throw a stone into a pond of water when the surface is still and smooth, you will see a circular wave proceed from the stone as its centre, quite to the sides of the pond; but the water does not proceed with the wave, it only rises and falls to form it in the different parts of its course; and the waves that follow the first, all make use of the same water with their predecessors.

But a wave in water is not indeed in all circumstances exactly like that in a cord; for, water being a fluid, and gravitating to the earth, it naturally runs from a higher place to a lower; therefore the parts of the wave in water do actually run a little both ways from its top towards its lower sides, which the parts of the wave in the cord cannot do. Thus, when it is high and standing water at Gravesend, the water 20 miles below has been running ebb, or towards the sea for an hour, or ever since it was high water there; but the water at London Bridge will run flood, or from the sea yet another hour, till it is high water or the top of the wave arrives at that bridge, and then it will have run ebb an hour at Gravesend, &c. &c. Now this motion of the water, occasion'd only by its gravity, or tendency to run from a higher place to a lower, is by no means so swift as the motion of the wave. It scarce exceeds perhaps two miles in an hour.

If it went, as the wave does, 20 miles an hour, no ships could ride at anchor in such a stream, nor boats row against it.

In common speech, indeed this current of the water both ways from the top of the wave, is called *the tide*; thus we say, *the tide runs strong, the tide runs at the rate of 1, 2, or 3 miles an hour, &c;* and, when we are at a part of the river behind the top of the wave, and find the water lower than high-water mark, and running towards the sea, we say, *the tide runs ebb;* and, when we are before the top of the wave, and find the water higher than low-water mark, and running from the sea, we say, *the tide runs flood;* but these expressions are only locally proper; for a tide, strictly speaking, is *one whole wave*, including all its parts higher and lower, and these waves succeed one another about twice in twenty-four hours.

This motion of the water, occasion'd by its gravity, will explain to you why the water near the mouth of rivers may be salter at high water than at low. Some of the salt water, as the tide wave enters the river, runs from its top and fore side, and mixes with the fresh, and also pushes it back up the river.

Supposing that the water commonly runs during the flood at the rate of two miles in an hour, and that the flood runs five hours, you see that it can bring at most into our canal only a quantity of water equal to the space included in the breadth of the canal, ten miles of its length, and the depth between low and high-water mark: Which is but a fourteenth part of what would be necessary to fill all the space between low and high-water mark for 140 miles, the whole length of the canal.

And indeed such a quantity of water as would fill that whole space, to run in and out every tide, must create so outrageous a current, as would do infinite damage to the shores, shipping, &c., and make the navigation of a river almost impracticable.

I have made this letter longer than I intended, and therefore reserve for another what I have farther to say on the subject of tides and rivers. I shall now only add, that I have not been exact in the numbers, because I would avoid perplexing you with minute calculations, my design at present being chiefly to give you distinct and clear ideas of the first principles.

.   .   .   .

Your affectionate Friend,
B. FRANKLIN.

DIRECTION OF RIVERS

TO

MISS MARY STEVENSON

[*September* 20, 1761]

MY DEAR FRIEND,

IT is, as you observed in our late conversation, a very general opinion, that *all rivers run into the sea,* or deposit their waters there. 'Tis a kind of audacity to call such general opinions in question, and may subject one to censure. But we must hazard something in what we think the cause of truth: and if we propose our objections modestly we shall tho' mistaken, deserve a censure less severe, than when we are both mistaken and insolent.

That some rivers run into the sea is beyond a doubt; such for instance, are the Amazones and, I think, the Oronoko and the Missisipi. The proof is, that their waters are fresh quite to the sea, and out to some distance from the land. Our question is, whether the fresh waters of those rivers whose beds are filled with salt water to a considerable distance up from the sea (as the Thames, the Delaware, and the rivers that communicate with Chesapeak Bay in Virginia) do ever arrive at the sea. And as I suspect they do not, I am now to acquaint you with my reasons; or, if they are not allow'd to be reasons, my conceptions at least of this matter.

The common supply of rivers is from springs, which draw

their origin from rain that has soak'd into the earth. The union of a number of springs forms a river. The waters, as they run, expos'd to the sun, air, and wind are continually evaporating. Hence in travelling one may often see where a river runs, by a long blueish mist over it, tho' we are at such a distance as not to see the river itself. The quantity of this evaporation is greater or less, in proportion to the surface exposed by the same quantity of water to those causes of evaporation. While the river runs in a narrow confined channel in the upper hilly country, only a small surface is exposed; a greater, as the river widens. Now, if a river ends in a lake, as some do, whereby its waters are spread so wide as that the evaporation is equal to the sum of all its springs, that lake will never overflow; and if instead of ending in a lake, it was drawn into greater length as a river, so as to expose a surface equal in the whole to that lake, the evaporation would be equal, and such river would end as a canal; when the ignorant might suppose, as they actually do in such cases, that the river loses itself by running under ground, whereas in truth it has run up into the air.

Now many rivers that are open to the sea widen much before they arrive at it, not merely by the additional waters they receive, but by having their course stopt by the opposing flood-tide; by being turned back twice in twenty-four hours, and by finding broader beds in the low flat countries to dilate themselves in. Hence the evaporation of the fresh water is proportionably increas'd; so that in some rivers it may equal the springs of supply. In such cases, the salt water comes up the river, and meets the fresh in that part where, if there were a wall or bank of earth across from side to side, the river would form a lake, fuller indeed at some times than at others, according to the seasons, but whose evaporation would, one time with another, be equal to its supply.

When the communication between the two kinds of water is open, this supposed wall of separation may be conceived as a moveable one, which is not only pushed some miles higher up the river by every flood tide from the sea, and carried down again as far by every tide of ebb, but which has even this space of vibration removed nearer to the sea in wet seasons, when the springs and brooks in the upper country are augmented by the falling rains, so as to swell the river, and farther from the sea in dry seasons.

Within a few miles above and below this moveable line of separation, the different waters mix a little, partly by their motion to and fro, and partly from the greater specific gravity of the salt water, which inclines it to run under the fresh, while the fresh water, being lighter, runs over the salt.

Cast your eye on the map of North America, and observe the Bay of Chesapeak, in Virginia, mentioned above; you will see, communicating with it by their mouths, the great rivers Susquehanah, Potowmack, Rappahanock, York, and James, besides a number of smaller streams, each as big as the Thames. It has been propos'd by philosophical writers, that to compute how much water any river discharges into the sea in a given time, we should measure its depth and swiftness at any part above the tide; as, for the Thames, at Kingston or Windsor. But can one imagine that if all the water of those vast rivers went to the sea, it would not first have pushed the salt water out of that narrow-mouthed Bay, and filled it with fresh? The Susquehanah alone would seem to be sufficient for this, if it were not for the loss by evaporation. And yet that Bay is salt quite up to Annapolis.

As to our other subject, the different degrees of heat imbibed from the sun's rays by cloths of different colours, since I cannot find the notes of my experiment to send you, I must give it as well as I can from memory.

But first let me mention an experiment you may easily make yourself. Walk but a quarter of an hour in your garden when the sun shines, with a part of your dress white, and a part black; then apply your hand to them alternately, and you will find a very great difference in their warmth. The black will be quite hot to the touch, the white still cool.

Another. Try to fire paper with a burning glass. If it is white, you will not easily burn it; but if you bring the focus to a black spot, or upon letters, written or printed, the paper will immediately be on fire under the letters.

Thus fullers and dyers find black cloths, of equal thickness with white ones, and hung out equally wet, dry in the sun much sooner than the white, being more readily heated by the sun's rays. It is the same before a fire; the heat of which sooner penetrates black stockings than white ones, and so is apt sooner to burn a man's shins. Also beer much sooner warms in a black mug set before the fire, than in a white one or in a bright silver tankard.

My experiment was this. I took a number of little square pieces of broad cloth from a taylor's pattern-card, of various colors. There were black, deep blue, lighter blue, green, purple red, yellow, white, and other colours, or shades of colours. I laid them all out upon the snow in a bright sunshiny morning. In a few hours (I cannot now be exact as to the time), the black, being warm'd most by the sun, was sunk so low as to be below the stroke of the sun's rays; the dark blue almost as low, the

[181]

lighter blue not quite so much as the dark, the other colours less as they were lighter; and the quite white remain'd on the surface of the snow, not having entred it at all.

What signifies philosophy that does not apply to some use? May we not learn from hence, that black clothes are not so fit to wear in a hot sunny climate or season, as white ones; because in such cloaths the body is more heated by the sun when we walk abroad, and are at the same time heated by the exercise, which double heat is apt to bring on putrid dangerous fevers? That soldiers and seamen, who must march and labour in the sun, should in the East or West Indies have an uniform of white? That summer hats, for men or women, should be white, as repelling that heat which gives headachs to many, and to some the fatal stroke that the French call the *coup de soleil?* That the ladies' summer hats, however, should be lined with black, as not reverberating on their faces those rays which are reflected upwards from the earth or water? That the putting a white cap of paper or linnen *within* the crown of a black hat, as some do, will not keep out the heat, tho' it would if placed *without?* That fruit-walls being black'd may receive so much heat from the sun in the daytime, as to continue warm in some degree thro' the night, and thereby preserve the fruit from frosts, or forward its growth? — with sundry other particulars of less or greater importance, that will occur from time to time to attentive minds? *I am*

Yours affectionately,
B. FRANKLIN.

SALT AND SALT WATER

PETER FRANKLIN

London, May 7, 1760.

SIR

.   .   .   .

IT has, indeed, as you observe, been the opinion of some very great naturalists, that the sea is salt only from the dissolution of mineral or rock salt, which its waters happened to meet with. But this opinion takes it for granted that all water was originally fresh, of which we can have no proof. I own I am inclined to a different opinion, and rather think all the water on this globe was originally salt, and that the fresh water we find in springs and rivers, is the produce of distillation. The sun raises the vapours from the sea, which form clouds, and fall in rain upon the land, and springs and rivers are formed of that rain. As to the rock salt found in mines, I conceive, that instead of communicating its saltness to the sea, it is itself drawn from the sea, and that of course the sea is now fresher than it was originally. This is only another effect of nature's distillery, and might be performed various ways.

It is evident from the quantities of sea-shells, and the bones and teeth of fishes found in high lands, that the sea has formerly covered them. Then, either the sea has been higher than it now is, and has fallen away from those high lands; or they have been lower than they are, and were lifted up out of the water to their present height, by some internal mighty force, such as we still feel some remains of, when whole continents are moved by earthquakes. In either case it may be supposed that large hollows, or valleys among hills, might be left filled with sea-water, which evaporating, and the fluid part drying away in a course of years, would leave the salt covering the bottom; and that salt, coming afterwards to be covered with earth from the neighbouring hills, could only be found by digging through that earth. Or, as we know from their effects, that there are deep fiery caverns under the earth, and even under the sea, if at any time the sea leaks into any of them, the fluid parts of the water must evaporate from that heat, and pass off through some volcano, while the salt remains, and by degrees, and continual accretion, becomes a great mass. Thus the cavern may at length be filled, and the volcano connected with it cease burning, as many it is said have done; and future miners, penetrating such cavern, find what we call a salt-mine. This is a fancy I had on visiting the salt-mines at *Northwich*, with my son. I send you a piece of the rock salt which he brought up with him out of the mine. . . . *I am, &c.*

B. FRANKLIN.

ORIGIN *of* NORTHEAST STORMS

TO

ALEXANDER SMALL

May 12, 1760.

DEAR SIR,

AGREEABLE to your request, I send you my reasons for thinking that our northeast storms in *North America* begin first, in point of time, in the south west parts: That is to say, the air in *Georgia*, the farthest of our colonies to the Southwest, begins to move southwesterly before the air of *Carolina*, which is the next colony northeastward; the air of *Carolina* has the same motion before the air of *Virginia*, which lies still more northeastward; and so on northeasterly through *Pennsylvania, New-York, New-England*, &c., quite to *Newfoundland*.

These northeast storms are generally very violent, continue sometimes two or three days, and often do considerable damage in the harbours along the coast. They are attended with thick clouds and rain.

What first gave me this idea, was the following circumstance. About twenty years ago, a few more or less, I cannot from my memory be certain, we were to have an eclipse of the moon at *Philadelphia*, on a *Friday* evening, about nine o'clock. I intended to observe it, but was prevented by a northeast storm, which came on about seven, with thick clouds as usual, that

[185]

quite obscured the whole hemisphere. Yet when the post brought us the *Boston* newspaper, giving an account of the effects of the same storm in those parts, I found the beginning of the eclipse had been well observed there, though Boston lies N.E. of *Philadelphia* about 400 miles. This puzzled me because the storm began with us so soon as to prevent any observation, and being a N. E. storm, I imagined it must have begun rather sooner in places farther to the northeastward than it did at *Philadelphia.* I therefore mentioned it in a letter to my brother, who lived at *Boston;* and he informed me the storm did not begin with them till near eleven o'clock, so that they had a good observation of the eclipse: And upon comparing all the other accounts I received from the several colonies, of the time of beginning of the same storm, and, since that of other storms of the same kind, I found the beginning to be always later the farther northeastward. I have not my notes with me here in *England,* and cannot, from memory, say the proportion of time to distance, but I think it is about an hour to every hundred miles.

From thence I formed an idea of the cause of these storms, which I would explain by a familiar instance or two. Suppose a long canal of water stopp'd at the end by a gate. The water is quite at rest till the gate is open, then it begins to move out through the gate; the water next the gate is first in motion, and moves towards the gate; the water next to that first water moves next, and so on successively, till the water at the head of the canal is in motion, which is last of all. In this case all the water moves indeed towards the gate, but the successive times of beginning motion are the contrary way, *viz.* from the gate backwards to the head of the canal. Again, suppose the air in a chamber at rest, no current through the room till you make a fire in the chimney. Immediately the air in the chimney, being rarefied by the fire, rises; the air next the chimney flows in to supply its place, moving towards the chimney; and, in consequence, the rest of the air successively, quite back to the door. Thus to produce our northeast storms, I suppose some great heat and rarefaction of the air in or about the Gulph of *Mexico;* the air thence rising has its place supplied by the next more northern, cooler, and therefore denser and heavier, air; that, being in motion, is followed by the next more northern air, &c. &c., in a successive current, to which current our coast and inland ridge of mountains give the direction of northeast, as they lie N. E. and S. W.

This I offer only as an hypothesis to account for this particular fact; and, perhaps, on farther examination, a better and truer may be found. I do not suppose all storms generated in the same manner. Our northwest thundergusts in *America* I know are not; but of them I have written my opinion fully in a paper which you have seen. *I am, etc.*

B. FRANKLIN.

EFFECT *of* OIL *on* WATER

TO

WILLIAM BROWNRIGG

London, November 7, 1773

DEAR SIR,

I THANK you for the remarks of your learned friend at Carlisle. I had, when a youth, read and smiled at Pliny's account of a practice among the seamen of his time, to still the waves in a storm by pouring oil into the sea; which he mentions, as well as the use made of oil by the diver; but the stilling a tempest by throwing vinegar into the air had escaped me. I think with your friend, that it has been of late too much the mode to slight the learning of the ancients. The learned, too, are apt to slight too much the knowledge of the vulgar. The cooling by evaporation was long an instance of the latter. This art of smoothing the waves by oil is an instance of both.

Perhaps you may not dislike to have an account of all I have heard, and learnt, and done in this way. Take it if you please as follows.

In 1757, being at sea in a fleet of ninety-six sail bound against Louisbourg, I observed the wakes of two of the ships to be remarkably smooth, while all the others were ruffled by the wind, which blew fresh. Being puzzled with the differing appearance, I at last pointed it out to our captain, and asked him the meaning of it. "The cooks," says he, "have, I suppose, been just emptying their greasy water through the scuppers, which has

[188]

greased the sides of those ships a little;" and this answer he gave me with an air of some little contempt, as to a person ignorant of what everybody else knew. In my own mind I at first slighted his solution, though I was not able to think of another; but recollecting what I had formerly read in Pliny, I resolved to make some experiment of the effect of oil on water, when I should have opportunity.

Afterwards being again at sea in 1762, I first observed the wonderful quietness of oil on agitated water, in the swinging glass lamp I made to hang up in the cabin, as described in my printed papers. This I was continually looking at and considering, as an appearance to me inexplicable. An old sea captain, then a passenger with me, thought little of it, supposing it an effect of the same kind with that of oil put on water to smooth it, which he said was a practice of the Bermudians when they would strike fish, which they could not see, if the surface of the water was ruffled by the wind. This practice I had never before heard of, and was obliged to him for the information; though I thought him mistaken as to the sameness of the experiment, the operations being different as well as the effects. In one case, the water is smooth till the oil is put on, and then becomes agitated. In the other it is agitated before the oil is applied, and then becomes smooth. The same gentleman told me, he had heard it was a practice with the fishermen of Lisbon when about to return into the river (if they saw before them too great a surf upon the bar, which they apprehended might fill their boats in passing) to empty a bottle or two of oil into the sea, which would suppress the breakers and allow them to pass safely. A confirmation of this I have not since had an opportunity of obtaining; but discoursing of it with another person, who had often been in the Mediterranean, I was informed, that the divers there, who, when under water in their business, need light, which the curling of the surface interrupts by the refractions of so many little waves, let a small quantity of oil now and then out of their mouths, which rising to the surface smooths it, and permits the light to come down to them. All these informations I at times revolved in my mind, and wondered to find no mention of them in our books of experimental philosophy.

At length being at Clapham, where there is, on the common, a large pond, which I observed one day to be very rough with the wind, I fetched out a cruet of oil, and dropped a little of it on the water. I saw it spread itself with surprising swiftness upon the surface; but the effect of smoothing the waves was not produced; for I had applied it first on the leeward side of the pond, where the waves were largest, and the wind drove my oil back upon the shore. I then went to the windward side where they began to form; and there the oil, though not more than a tea spoonful, produced an instant calm over a space several yards square, which spread amazingly, and extended itself gradually till it reached the lee side, making all that quarter of the pond, perhaps half an acre, as smooth as a looking-glass.

After this I contrived to take with me, whenever I went into the country, a little oil in the upper hollow joint of my bamboo cane, with which I might repeat the experiment as opportunity should offer, and I found it constantly to succeed.

In these experiments, one circumstance struck me with particular surprise. This was the sudden, wide, and forcible spreading of a drop of oil on the face of the water, which I do not know that anybody has hitherto considered. If a drop of oil is put on a highly polished marble table, or on a looking-glass that lies horizontally, the drop remains in its place, spreading very little. But, when put on water, it spreads instantly, many feet round, becoming so thin as to produce the prismatic colors, for a considerable space, and beyond them so much thinner as to be invisible, except in its effect of smoothing the waves at a much greater distance. It seems as if a mutual repulsion between its particles took place as soon as it touched the water, and a repulsion so strong as to act on other bodies swimming on the surface, as straw, leaves, chips, &c. forcing them to recede every way from the drop, as from a center, leaving a large, clear space. The quantity of this force, and the distance to which it will operate, I have not yet ascertained; but I think it a curious inquiry, and I wish to understand whence it arises.

In our journey to the North, when we had the pleasure of seeing you at Ormathwaite, we visited the celebrated Mr. Smeaton, near Leeds. Being about to show him the smoothing experiment on a little pond near his house, an ingenious pupil of his, Mr. Jessop, then present, told us of an odd appearance on that pond, which had lately occurred to him. He was about to clean a little cup in which he kept oil, and he threw upon the water some flies that had been drowned in the oil. These flies presently began to move, and turned round on the water very rapidly, as if they were vigorously alive, though on examination he found they were not so. I immediately concluded that the motion was occasioned by the power of the repulsion above mentioned, and that the oil issuing gradually from the spungy body of the fly continued the motion. He found some more flies drowned in oil, with which the experiment was repeated before us. To show that it was not any effect of life recovered by the flies, I imitated it by little bits of oiled chips and paper, cut in the form of a comma, of the size of a common fly; when the stream of repelling particles issuing from the point made the comma turn round the contrary way. This is not a chamber experiment; for it cannot be well repeated in a bowl or dish of water on a table. A considerable surface of water is necessary to give room for the expansion of a small quantity of oil. In a dish of water, if the smallest drop of oil be let fall in the middle, the whole surface is presently covered with a thin greasy film proceeding from the drop; but as soon as that film has reached the sides of the dish, no more will issue from the drop, but it remains in the form of oil, the sides of the dish putting a stop to its dissipation by prohibiting the farther expansion of the film.

Our friend Sir John Pringle, being soon after in Scotland, learned there, that those employed in the herring fishery could at a distance see where the shoals of herrings were, by the smoothness of the water over them, which might possibly be occasioned, he thought, by some oiliness proceeding from their bodies.

A gentleman from Rhode Island told me, it had been remarked, that the harbour of Newport was ever smooth while any whaling vessels were in it; which probably arose from hence, that the blubber which they sometimes bring loose in the hold, or the leakage of their barrels, might afford some oil, to mix with that water, which from time to time they pump out, to keep their vessel free, and that some oil might spread over the surface of the water in the harbour, and prevent the forming of any waves.

This prevention I would thus endeavor to explain.

There seems to be no natural repulsion between water and

air, such as to keep them from coming into contact with each other. Hence we find a quantity of air in water; and if we extract it by means of the air-pump, the same water, again exposed to the air, will soon imbibe an equal quantity.

Therefore air in motion, which is wind, in passing over the smooth surface of water, may rub, as it were, upon that surface, and raise it into wrinkles, which, if the wind continues, are the elements of future waves.

The smallest wave once raised does not immediately subside, and leave the neighbouring water quiet; but in subsiding raises nearly as much of the water next to it, the friction of the parts making little difference. Thus a stone dropped in a pool raises first a single wave round itself; and leaves it, by sinking to the bottom; but that first wave subsiding raises a second, a second a third, and so on in circles to a great extent.

A small power continually operating will produce a great action. A finger applied to a weighty suspended bell can at first move it but little; if repeatedly applied, though with no greater strength, the motion increases till the bell swings to its utmost height, and with a force that cannot be resisted by the whole strength of the arm and body. Thus the small first-raised waves, being continually acted upon by the wind, are, though the wind does not increase in strength, continually increased in magnitude, rising higher and extending their basis, so as to include a vast mass of water in each wave, which in its motion acts with great violence.

But if there be a mutual repulsion between the particles of oil, and no attraction between oil and water, oil dropped on water will not be held together by adhesion to the spot whereon it falls; it will not be imbibed by the water; it will be at liberty to expand itself; and it will spread on a surface, that besides being smooth to the most perfect degree of polish, prevents, perhaps by repelling the oil, all immediate contact, keeping it at a minute distance from itself; and the expansion will continue till the mutual repulsion between the particles of the oil is weakened and reduced to nothing by their distance.

Now I imagine that the wind, blowing over water thus covered with a film of oil, cannot easily *catch* upon it, so as to raise the first wrinkles, but slides over it, and leaves it smooth as it finds it. It moves a little the oil indeed, which being between it and the water, serves it to slide with, and prevents friction, as oil does between those parts of a machine, that would otherwise rub hard together. Hence the oil dropped on the windward side of a pond proceeds gradually to leeward, as may be seen by the smoothness it carries with it, quite to the opposite side. For the wind being thus prevented from raising the first wrinkles, that I call the elements of waves, cannot produce waves, which are to be made by continually acting upon, and enlarging those elements, and thus the whole pond is calmed.

Totally therefore we might suppress the waves in any required place, if we could come at the windward place where they take their rise. This in the ocean can seldom if ever be done. But perhaps, something may be done on particular occasions, to moderate the violence of the waves when we are in the midst of them, and prevent their breaking where that would be inconvenient.

For, when the wind blows fresh, there are continually rising on the back of every great wave a number of small ones, which roughen its surface, and give the wind hold, as it were, to push it with greater force. This hold is diminished, by preventing the generation of those small ones. And possibly too, when a wave's surface is oiled, the wind, in passing over it, may rather in some degree press it down, and contribute to prevent its rising again, instead of promoting it.

This, as mere conjecture, would have little weight, if the apparent effects of pouring oil into the midst of waves were not considerable, and as yet not otherwise accounted for.

When the wind blows so fresh, as that the waves are not sufficiently quick in obeying its impulse, their tops being thinner and lighter are pushed forward, broken, and turned over in a white foam. Common waves lift a vessel without entering it; but these when large sometimes break above and pour over it, doing great damage.

That this effect might in any degree be prevented, or the height and violence of waves in the sea moderated, we had no certain account; Pliny's authority for the practice of seamen in his time being slighted. But discoursing lately on this subject with his Excellency Count Bentinck, of Holland, his son the Honourable Captain Bentinck, and the learned Professor Allemand, (to all whom I showed the experiment of smoothing in a windy day the large piece of water at the head of the Green Park,) a letter was mentioned, which had been received by the Count from Batavia, relative to the saving of a Dutch ship in a storm by pouring oil into the sea. I much desired to see that letter, and a copy of it was promised me, which I afterward received.

Extract of a letter from Mr. Tengnagel to Count Bentinck, dated at Batavia 5 January, 1770.

"Near the islands Paul and Amsterdam, we met with a

storm, which had nothing particular in it worthy of being communicated to you, except that the captain found himself obliged for greater safety in wearing the ship, to pour oil into the sea, to prevent the waves breaking over her, which had an excellent effect, and succeeded in preserving us. As he poured out but a little at a time, the East India Company owes perhaps its ship to only six demi-ames of oil-olive. I was present upon deck when this was done; and I should not have mentioned this circumstance to you, but that we have found people here so prejudiced against the experiment, as to make it necessary for the officers on board and myself to give a certificate of the truth on this head, of which we made no difficulty."

On this occasion, I mentioned to Captain Bentinck a thought which had occurred to me in reading the voyages of our late circumnavigators, particularly where accounts are given of pleasant and fertile islands which they much desired to land upon, when sickness made it more necessary, but could not effect a landing through a violent surf breaking on the shore, which rendered it impracticable. My idea was, that possibly by sailing to and fro at some distance from such lee-shore, continually pouring oil into the sea, the waves might be so much depressed, and lessened before they reached the shore, as to abate the height and violence of the surf, and permit a landing; which, in such circumstances, was a point of sufficient importance to justify the expense of the oil that might be requisite for the purpose.

. . . .

I conceive, that the operation of oil on water is, first, to prevent the raising of new waves by the wind; and, secondly, to prevent its pushing those before raised with such force, and consequently their continuance of the same repeated height, as they would have done, if their surface were not oiled. But oil will not prevent waves being raised by another power, by a stone, for instance, falling into a still pool; for they then rise by the mechanical impulse of the stone, which the greasiness on the surrounding water cannot lessen or prevent, as it can prevent the winds catching the surface and raising it into waves. Now waves once raised, whether by the wind or any other power, have the same mechanical operation, by which they continue to rise and fall, as a *pendulum* will continue to swing a long time after the force ceases to act by which the motion was first produced; that motion will, however, cease in time; but time is necessary. Therefore, though oil spread on an agitated sea may weaken the push of the wind on those waves whose surfaces are covered by it, and so, by receiving less fresh impulse, they may gradually subside; yet a considerable time, or a distance through which they will take time to move, may be necessary to make the effect sensible on any shore in a diminution of the surf; for we know, that, when wind ceases suddenly, the waves it has raised do not as suddenly subside, but settle gradually, and are not quite down till after the wind has ceased. So, though we should, by oiling them, take off the effect of wind on waves already raised, it is not to be expected that those waves should be instantly levelled. The motion they have received will, for some time, continue; and, if the shore is not far distant, they arrive there so soon, that their effect upon it will not be visibly diminished.

.   .   .   .

Your most obedient humble servant,

B. FRANKLIN.

[197]

SPOUTS AND WHIRLWINDS

TO

JOHN PERKINS

Philada, Feb. 4, 1753.

DEAR SIR,

. . . .

I AGREE with you, that by means of a vacuum in a whirl-wind, water cannot be suppos'd to rise in large masses to the region of the clouds: for the pressure of the surrounding atmosphere could not force it up in a continu'd body or column, to a much greater height than thirty feet. But if there really is a vacuum in the center, or near the axis of whirlwinds, then I think water may rise in such vacuum to that height, or to less height, as the vacuum may be less perfect.

I had not read Stuart's Acc^t. in the *Transactions,* for many years before the receipt of your letter, and had quite forgot it; but now, on viewing his drafts, and considering his descriptions, I think they seem to favour my *hypothesis:* For he describes and draws columns of water, of various heights, terminating abruptly at the top, exactly as water would do when forc'd up by the pressure of the atmosphere into an exhausted tube.

I must, however, no longer call it my *hypothesis,* since I find Stuart had the same thought, tho' somewhat obscurely express'd, where he says, "he imagines this phænomenon may be solv'd by suction (improperly so called), or rather pulsion, as in the application of a cupping-glass to the flesh, the air being first voided by the kindled flax."

In my paper, I supposed a whirlwind and a spout to be the same thing, and to proceed from the same cause; the only difference between them being, that the one passes over land, the other over water. I find also in the *Transactions*, that M. de la Pryme was of the same opinion; for he there describes two spouts, as he calls them, which were seen at different times, at Hatfield in Yorkshire, whose Appearances in the air were the same with those of the spouts at sea, and effects the same with those of real whirlwinds.

Whirlwinds have generally a progressive, as well as a circular motion . . . Water-spouts have likewise a progressive motion; this is sometimes greater, and sometimes less; in some violent, in others barely perceivable. . . .

Whirlwinds generally arise after calms and great heats: The same is observ'd of water-spouts, which are therefore most frequent in the warm latitudes. The spout that happen'd in cold weather, in the Downs, describ'd by Mr. Gordon, in the *Transactions*, was for that reason thought extraordinary; but he remarks withal, that the weather, tho' cold when the spout appeared, was soon after much colder; as we find it commonly less warm after a whirlwind.

You agree that the wind blows every way towards a whirlwind, from a large space round. An intelligent whaleman, of Nantucket, informed me, that three of their vessels, which were out in search of whales, happening to be becalmed lay in sight of each other at about a league distance: if I remember right, nearly forming a triangle; after some time, a water-spout appeared near the middle of the triangle, when a brisk breeze of wind also sprang up, and every vessel made sail; and then it appeared to them all, by the setting of the sails, and the course each vessel stood, that the spout was to Leeward of every one of them; and they all declar'd it to have been so, when they happen'd afterwards in company, and came to confer about it. So that in this particular likewise, whirlwinds and water-spouts agree.

But if that which appears a water-spout at sea, does sometimes in its progressive motion, meet with and pass over land, and there produce all the phenomena and effects of a whirlwind, it should thence seem still more evident, that a whirlwind and a spout are the same. I send you, herewith, a letter from an ingenious physician of my acquaintance, which gives one instance of this, that fell within his observation.

A fluid, moving from all points horizontally, towards a center, must, at that center, either ascend or descend. Water being in a tub, if a hole be open'd in the middle of the bottom, will flow from all sides to the center, and there descend in a whirl. But air flowing on and near the surface of land or water, from all sides toward a center, must at that center ascend; the land or water hindering its descent.

If these concentring currents of air be in the upper region, they may indeed descend in the spout or whirlwind; but then, when the united current reach'd the earth or water it would spread, and, probably, blow every way *from* the center. There may be whirlwinds of both kinds, but, from the commonly observ'd effects, I suspect the rising one to be the most common; when the upper air descends, 'tis, perhaps, in a greater body extending wider, as in our thunder-gusts, and without much whirling; and, when air descends in a spout, or whirlwind, I should rather expect it would press the roof of a house *inwards,* or force *in* the tiles, shingles, or thatch, force a boat down into the water, or a piece of timber into the earth, than that it would lift them up, and carry them away.

It has so happen'd, that I have not met with any accounts of spouts, that certainly descended; I suspect they are not frequent. . . .

The augmentation of the cloud, which, as I am inform'd, is generally if not always the case, during a spout, seems to show an ascent rather than a descent of the matter of which such cloud is composed. For a descending spout, one would expect should diminish a cloud. I own, however, that descending cold air, may, by condensing the vapours in a lower region, form and increase clouds; which, I think, is generally the case in our common thunder-gusts, and, therefore, do not lay great stress on this argum^t.

Whirlwinds and spouts are not always tho' most commonly in the day time. The terrible whirlwind, which damag'd a great part of Rome, June 11. 1749 happen'd in the night of that day. The same was supposed to have been first a spout, for it is said to be beyond doubt, that it gathered in the neighbouring sea, as it could be tracked from Ostia to Rome. I find this in Père Boschovich's Acc^t of it, as abridg'd in the *Monthly Review* for December 1750:

In that Acct, the whirlwind is said to have appeared as a very black, long, and lofty cloud, discoverable, notwithstanding the darkness of the night, by its continually lightning or emitting flashes on all sides, pushing along with a surprizing swiftness, and within 3 or 4 feet of the ground. Its general effects on houses were, stripping off the roofs, blowing away chimneys, breaking doors and windows, *forcing up the floors, and unpaving the rooms,* (some of these effects seem to agree well with a supposed vacuum in the center of the whirlwind,) and the very rafters of the houses were broke and dispersed, and even hurled against houses at a considerable distance, &c.

It seems, by an expression of Père Boschovich's, as if the wind blew from all sides towards this whirlwind; for having carefully observ'd its effects, he concludes of all whirlwinds, "that their Motion is circular, and their Action attractive."

He observes, on a number of histories of whirlwinds, &c., "that a common effect of them is to carry up into the air, tiles, stones and animals themselves, which happen to be in their course, and all kinds of bodies unexceptionably, throwing them to a considerable distance, with great impetuosity."

Such effects seem to show a rising current of air.

I will endeavour to explain my conceptions of this matter, by figures representing a plan, and an elevation of a spout or whirlwind.

I would only first beg to be allowed two or three positions, mentioned in my former paper.

1. That the lower region of air is often more heated, and so more rarified, than the upper; consequently, specifically lighter. The coldness of the upper region is manifested by the hail, which sometimes falls from it in a hot day.

2. That heated air may be very moist, and yet the moisture so equally diffus'd and rarified, as not to be visible, till colder air mixes with it, when it condenses, and becomes visible. Thus our breath, invisible in summer, becomes visible in winter.

Now let us suppose a tract of land or sea of perhaps 60 miles square, unscreen'd by clouds, and unfann'd by winds, during great part of a summer's day, or it may be for several days successively, till 'tis violently heated, together with the lower region of air in contact with it, so that the said lower air becomes specifically lighter than the superincumbent higher region of the atmosphere, in which the clouds commonly float; let us suppose, also, that the air surrounding this tract has not been so much heated during those days, and therefore remains heavier. The consequence of this should be, as I imagine, that the heated, lighter air, being press'd on all sides, must ascend, and the heavier descend; and as this rising cannot be in all parts, or the whole area of the tract at once, for that would leave too extensive a vacuum, the rising will begin precisely in that column that happens to be the lightest, or most rarified; and the warm air will flow horizontally from all points to this column, where the several currents meeting, and joining to rise, a whirl is naturally formed, in the same manner as a whirl is formed in the tub of water, by the descending fluid flowing from all sides of the tub to the hole in the center.

And as the several currents arrive at this central rising column with a considerable degree of horizontal motion, they cannot suddenly change it to a vertical motion, therefore as they gradually, in approaching the whirl decline from right to curve, or circular lines, so having join'd the whirl, they *ascend* by a spiral motion, in the same manner as the water *descends* spirally thro' the hole in the tub before mentioned.

Lastly, as the lower air, and nearest the surface, is most rarified by the heat of the sun, that air is most acted on by the pressure of the surrounding cold and heavy air, which is to take its place; consequently its motion tow'ds the whirl is swiftest, and so the force of the lower part of the whirl, or trump, strongest, and the centrifugal force of its particles greatest; and hence the vacuum round the axis of the whirl should be greatest near the earth or sea, and be gradually diminish'd as it approaches the region of the clouds, till it ends in a point, as at [A, in Fig. II,] forming a long and sharp cone.

In Fig. I, which is a plan or ground-plot of a whirlwind, the circle *V* represents the central vacuum.

Between *a a a a* and *b b b b*, I suppose a body of air, condens'd strongly, by the pressure of the currents moving towards it from all sides without, and by its centrifugal force from within, moving round with prodigious swiftness, (having, as it were, the Momenta of all the currents, ——> ——> ——> ——>, united in itself), and with a power equal to its swiftness and density.

It is this whirling body of air between *a a a a* and *b b b b* that rises spirally; by its force it tears buildings to pieces, twists up great trees by the roots, &c., and, by its spiral motion, raises the fragments so high, till the pressure of the surrounding and approaching currents diminishing can no longer confine them to the circle, or their own centrifugal force, encreasing, grows too strong for such pressure, when they fly off in tangent lines, as stones out of a sling, and fall on all sides, and at great distances.

If it happens at sea, the water between *a a a a* and *b b b b* will be violently agitated and driven about, and parts of it raised with the spiral current, and thrown about so as to form a bush-like appearance.

This circle is of various diameters, sometimes very large.

If the vacuum passes over water the water may rise in it in a body or column, to near the height of 32 feet.

If it passes over houses, it may burst their windows or walls

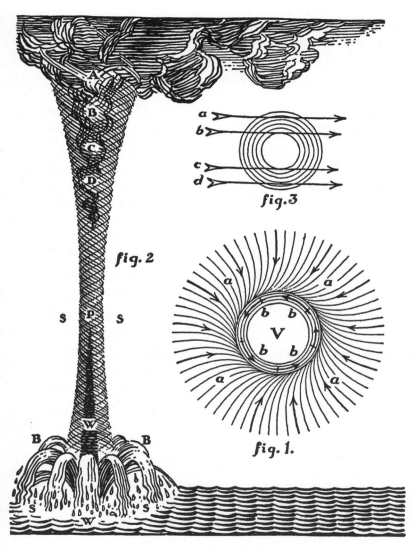

WHIRLWIND AND WATERSPOUT

outwards, pluck off the roofs and blow up the floors, by the sudden rarefaction of the air contain'd within such buildings, the outward pressure of the atmosphere being suddenly taken off. So the stop'd bottle of air bursts under the exhausted receiver of the air pump.

Fig. II is to represent the elevation of a water-spout, wherein I suppose *P* to be the cone, at first a vacuum, till *W W*, the rising column of water, has fill'd so much of it. *S S S S*, the spiral whirl of air, surrounding the vacuum, and continu'd higher in a close column after the vacuum ends in the point *P*, till it reach the cool region of the air. *B B*, the bush, describ'd by Stuart, surrounding the foot of the column of water.

Now I suppose this whirl of air will, at first, be as invisible as the air itself, tho' reaching in reality from the water to the region of cool air, in which our low summer thunder-clouds commonly float; but presently it will become visible at its extremities. *At its lower end,* by the agitation of the water under the whirling part of the circle, between *P* and *S*, forming Stuart's bush, and by the swelling and rising of the water in the beginning vacuum, which is at first a small, low, broad cone, whose top gradually rises and sharpens, as the force of the whirl increases. *At its upper end* it becomes visible, by the warm air brought up to the cooler region, where its moisture begins to be condens'd into thick vapour by the cold, and is seen first at *A*, the highest part, which being now cool'd, condenses what rises next at *B*, which condenses that at *C*, and that condenses what is rising at *D*. The cold operating by the contact of the vapours faster in a right line downwards, than the vapours themselves can climb in a spiral line upwards; they climb, however, and, as by continual addition they grow denser, and consequently their centrifugal force greater, and being risen above the concentrating currents that compose the whirl, they flie off, spread and form a cloud.

It seems easy to conceive, how by this successive condensation from above, the spout appears to drop or descend from the cloud, tho' the materials of which it is composed are all the while ascending.

The condensation of the moisture, contain'd in so great a quantity of warm air as may be suppos'd to rise in a short time in this prodigiously rapid whirl, is, perhaps sufficient to form a great extent of a cloud, tho' the spout should be over land, as those at Hatfield; and if the land happens not to be very dusty, perhaps the lower part of the spout will scarce become visible at all; tho' the upper, or what is commonly call'd the descending part, be very distinctly seen.

The same may happen at sea, in case the whirl is not violent enough to make a high vacuum, and raise the column, &c. In such case, the upper part $A B C D$ only will be visible, and the bush perhaps below.

But if the whirl be strong, and there be much dust on the land, and the column $W W$ be rais'd from the water, then the lower part becomes visible, and sometimes even united to the upper part. For the dust may be carried up in the spiral whirl, till it reach the region where the vapour is condens'd, and rise with that even to the clouds. And the friction of the whirling air, on the sides of the column $W W$, may detach great quantities of its water, break it into drops, and carry them up in the spiral whirl, mix'd with the air; the heavier drops may indeed fly off, and fall in a shower, round the spout; but much of it will be broken into vapour, yet visible; and thus in both cases by dust at land, and by water at sea, the whole tube may be darkened and render'd visible.

As the whirl weakens, the tube may (in appearance) separate in the middle; the column of water subsiding, and the superior condens'd part drawing up to the cloud. Yet still the tube or whirl of air, may remain entire, the middle only becoming invisible, as not containing visible matter.

Dr. Stuart says, "It was observable of all the spouts he saw, but more perceptible of the great one, that towards the end it began to appear like a hollow canal, only black in the borders, but white in the middle; and, tho' at first it was altogether black and opaque, yet now one could very distinctly perceive the sea water to fly up along the middle of this canal, as smoak up a chimney."

And Dr. Mather, describing a whirlwind, says, "A thick dark small cloud arose, with a pillar of light in it, of about 8 or 10 feet diam., and passed along the ground in a tract not wider than a street, horribly tearing up trees by the roots, blowing them up on the air like feathers, and throwing up stones of great weight to a considerable height in the air," &c.

These acc^{ts}, the one of water-spouts, the other of a whirlwind, seem in this particular to agree; what one gentleman describes as a tube, black in the borders, and white in the middle; the other calls a black cloud, with a pillar of light in it; the latter expression has only a little more of the marvelous, but the thing is the same. And it seems not very difficult to understand. When Dr. Stuart's spouts were full charg'd; that is, when the whirling pipe of air was filled between *a a a a* and *b b b b*, Fig. 1, with quantities of drops, and vapour torn off from the column *W W*, Fig. 2, the whole was render'd so dark as that it could not be seen thro', nor the spiral ascending motion discover'd; but when the quantity ascending lessen'd, the pipe became more transparent, and the ascending motion visible. For, by inspection of this figure, [Fig. 3,] representing a section of our spout, with the vacuum in the middle, it is plain, that if we look at such a hollow pipe, in the direction of the arrows, and suppose opacous particles to be equally mix'd in the space between the two circular lines, both the part between the arrows *a* and *b*, and that between the arrows *c* and *d*, will appear much darker than that between *b* and *c*, as there must be many more of those opaque particles in the line of vision, across the sides, than across the middle. It is thus, that a hair in a microscope evidently appears to be a pipe, the sides shewing darker than the middle. Dr. Mather's whirl was probably fill'd with dust, the sides were very dark, but the vacuum within rendering the middle more transparent, he calls it a pillar of light.

It was in this more transparent part between *b* and *c*, that Stuart could see the spiral motion of the vapours, whose lines on the nearest and farthest side of the transparent part crossing each other, represented smoke ascending in a chimney; for the quantity being still too great in the line of sight thro' the sides of the tube, the motion could not be discover'd there, and so they represented the solid sides of the chimney.

When the vapours reach in the pipe from the clouds near to the earth, it is no wonder now to those who understand electricity, that flashes of lightning should descend by the spout, as in that at Rome.

But you object, if water may be thus carried into the clouds, why have we no salt rains? The objection is strong and reasonable, and I know not whether I can answer it to your satisfaction. I never heard but of one salt rain, and that was where a spout passed pretty near a ship; so I suppose it to be only the drops thrown off from the spout, by the centrifugal force (as the birds were at Hatfield), when they had been carried so high as to be above, or to be too strongly centrifugal for, the pressure of the concurring winds surrounding it. And indeed I believe there can be no other kind of salt rain; for it has pleased the goodness of God so to order it, that the particles of air will not attract the particles of salt, tho' they strongly attract water.

Hence, tho' all metals, even gold, may be united with air, and render'd volatile, salt remains fix'd in the fire, and no heat can force it up to any considerable height, or oblige the air to hold it. Hence when salt rises as it will a little way, into air with water, there is instantly a separation made; the particles of water adhere to the air, and the particles of salt fall down again, as if repell'd and forc'd off from the water by some power in the air; or, as some metals, dissolv'd in a proper menstruum, will quit the solvent when other matter approaches, and adhere to that, so the water quits the salt, and embraces the air; but air will not embrace the salt, and quit the water. Otherwise our rains would indeed be salt, and every tree and plant on the face of the earth be destroy'd, with all the animals that depend on them for subsistence. He who hath proportioned and given proper qualities to all things, was not unmindful of this. Let us adore HIM with Praise and Thanksgiving!

By some accounts of seamen, it seems the column of water, W W, sometimes falls suddenly; and if it be, as some say, 15 or 20 yds diameter, it must fall with great force, and they may well fear for their ships. By one acc^t, in the *Transactions*, of a spout that fell at Coln in Lancashire, one would think the column is sometimes lifted off from the water, and carried over land, and there let fall in a body; but this, I suppose, happens rarely.

Stuart describes his spouts as appearing no bigger than a mast, and sometimes less; but they were at a league and half distance.

I think I formerly read in Dampier, or some other Voyager, that a spout, in its progressive motion, went over a ship becalmed on the coast of Guinea, and first threw her down on one side, carrying away her foremast, then suddenly whipt her up, and threw her down on the other side, carrying away her mizen-mast, and the whole was over in an instant. I suppose the first mischief was done by the fore side of the whirl, the latter by the hinder side, their motion being contrary.

I suppose a whirlwind, or spout, may be stationary, when the concurring winds; are equal; but if unequal, the whirl acquires a progressive motion, in the direction of the strongest pressure.

When the wind that gives the progressive motion becomes stronger below than above, or above than below, the spout will be bent, and, the cause ceasing, straiten again.

. . . .

Here you have my method of accounting for the principal phænomena, which I submit to your candid examination.

If my hypothesis is not the truth itself it is least as naked: For I have not with some of our learned moderns, disguis'd my nonsense in Greek, cloth'd it in algebra or adorn'd it with fluxions. You have it in puris naturalibus. And as I now seem to have almost written a book, instead of a letter, you will think it high time I should conclude; which I beg leave to do, with assuring you, that *I am, most sincerely, D*ʳ *Sir, etc.*

B. FRANKLIN.

SUN SPOTS

TO

HUMPHRY MARSHALL

London, February 14, 1773.

SIR,

A CONSIDERABLE time after its arrival, I received the box of seeds you sent me the beginning of last year, with your observations on spots of the sun. The seeds I distributed among some of my friends who are curious; accept my thankful acknowledgments for them. The observations I communicated to our astronomers of the Royal Society, who are much pleased with them, and hand them about from one to another; so that I have had little opportunity of examining them myself, they not being yet returned to me.

Here are various opinions about the solar spots. Some think them vast clouds of smoke and soot arising from the consuming fuel on the surface, which at length take fire again on their edges, consuming and daily diminishing till they totally disappear. Others think them spots of the surface, in which the fire has been extinguished, and which by degrees is rekindled. It is however remarkable, that, though large spots are seen gradually to become small ones, no one has observed a small spot gradually become a large one; at least I do not remember to have met with such an observation. If this be so, it should seem they are suddenly formed of their full size; and perhaps, if there were more such constant and diligent observers as you, some might happen to be observing at the instant such a spot was formed, when the appearances might give some ground of conjecture by what means they were formed.

The professor of astronomy at Glasgow, Dr. Wilson, has a new hypothesis. It is this; that the sun is a globe of solid matter, all combustible, perhaps, but whose surface only is actually on fire to a certain depth, and all below that depth unkindled, like a log of wood, whose surface to half an inch deep may be burning coal, while all within remains wood. Then he supposes, by some explosion similar to our earthquakes, the burning part may be blown away from a particular district, leaving bare the unkindled part below, which then appears a spot, and only lessens as the fluid burning matter by degrees flows in upon it on all sides, and at last covers or rekindles it.

He founds this opinion on certain appearances of the edges of the spots as they turn under the sun's disk, or emerge again on the other side; for, if there are such hollows in the sun's face as he supposes, and the bright border round their edges be the fluid burning matter flowing down the banks into the hollow, it will follow, that, while a spot is in the middle of the sun's disk, the eye looking directly upon the whole, may discern that border all round; but when the hollow is moved round to near the edge of the disk, then, though the eye which now views it aslant can see full the farthest bank, yet that which is nearest is hidden, and not to be distinguished; and when the same spot comes to emerge again on the other side of the sun, the bank which before was visible is now concealed, and that concealed which before was visible, gradually changing, however, till the spot reaches the middle of the disk, when the bank all round may be seen as before. Perhaps your telescope may be scarce strong enough to observe this. If it is, I wish to know whether you find the same appearances. When your observations are returned to me, and I have considered them, I shall lodge them among the papers of the Society, and let you know their sentiments.

With great esteem and regard, I am, &c.

B. FRANKLIN.

CONDUCTORS AND
NON-CONDUCTORS

TO

CADWALLADER COLDEN

Philadelphia, April 23, '52.

SIR,

IN considering your fav^r of the 16th past, I recollected my having wrote you answers to some queries concerning the difference between El *per se*, and Non-Els, and the effects of air in El. experiments, which, I apprehend, you may not have received. The date I have forgot.

We have been us'd to call those bodies Els *per se*, which would not conduct the electric fluid; we once imagin'd that only such bodies contain'd that fluid; afterwards that they contain'd none of it, [and only educed it from other bodies;] but farther experiments shew'd our mistakes. It is to be found in all matter we know of; and the distinction of Els *per se*, and Non-Els, should now be dropt as improper, and that of *Cond^{rs}* and *Non Cond^{rs}* assum'd in its place, as I mention'd in those answers.

I do not remember any experiment by which it appear'd that high rectified spirit will not conduct; perhaps you have made such. This I know, that wax, rosin, brimstone, and even glass, commonly reputed electrics *per se*, will, when in a fluid state, conduct pretty well. Glass will do it, when only red-hot. So that my former position, that only metals and water were conductors, and other bodies more or less such, as they partook of metal or moisture, was too general.

Your conception of the El. fluid, that it is incomparably more subtile than air, is undoubtedly just. It pervades dense matter with the greatest ease. But it does not seem to mix or incorporate willingly with meer air, as it does with other matter. It will not quit common matter to join with air. Air obstructs in some degree its motion. An electric atmosphere cannot be communicated at so great a distance, thro' intervening air, by far, as thro' a vacuum. Who knows then, but there may be, as the ancients thought, a region of this fire above our atmosphere, prevented by our air, and its own too great distance for attraction, from joining our earth? Perhaps where the atmosphere is rarest, this fluid may be densest, and nearer the earth where the atmosphere grows denser, this fluid may be rarer, yet some of it be low enough to attach itself to our highest clouds and thence they becoming electrified may be attracted by, and descend towards the earth, and discharge their watry contents, together with that ethereal fire. Perhaps the Auroræ Boreales are currents of this fluid in its own region, above our atmosphere, becoming from their motion visible. There is no end to conjectures. As yet we are but novices in this branch of natural knowledge.

You mention several differences of salts in electrical experiments. Were they all equally dry? Salt is apt to acquire moisture from a moist air, and some sorts more than others. When perfectly dry'd by lying before a fire, or on a stove, none that I have try'd will conduct any better than so much glass.

New flannel, if dry and warm, will draw the El. fluid from non-electrics, as well as that which has been worn.

I wish you had the convenience of trying the experiments you seem to have such expectations from, upon various kinds of spirits, salts, earths &c. Frequently, in a variety of exp^{ts} tho' we miss what we expected to find, yet something valuable turns out, something surprising, and instructing, tho' unthought of. I am glad your piece on the Principles of Action in Matter, with the explanations, is likely soon to appear. I hope it may be printed correctly. Tracts on uncommon subjects, when the author is at a distance frequently suffer much in the press, thro' the ignorance of the workmen. I think my letters were almost as fairly wrote, as print itself, yet they were publish'd with several errata that render particular parts quite unintelligible.

I thank you for communicating the illustration of the Theorem concerning Light. It is very curious. But I must own I am much in the *Dark* about *Light*. I am not satisfy'd with the doctrine that supposes particles of matter call'd light, continually driven off from the sun's surface, with a swiftness so prodigious! Must not the smallest particle conceivable have, with such a motion, a force exceeding that of a 24 pounder, discharg'd from a cannon? Must not the sun diminish exceedingly by such a waste of matter, and the planets, instead of drawing nearer to him, as some have feared, recede to greater distances, thro' the lessened attraction? Yet these particles, with this amazing motion, will not drive before them, or remove, the least and lightest dust they meet with. And the sun for aught we know continues of his ancient dimensions, and his attendants move in their ancient orbits.

May not all the phænomena of light be more conveniently

solved, by supposing universal space filled with a subtle elastic fluid, which, when at rest, is not visible, but whose vibrations affect that fine sense the eye, as those of air do the grosser organs of the ear? We do not, in the case of sound, imagine that any sonorous particles are thrown off from a bell, for instance, and fly in strait lines to the ear; why must we believe that luminous particles leave the sun and proceed to the eye? Some diamonds, if rubbed, shine in the dark, without losing any part of their matter. I can make an electrical spark as big as the flame of a candle, much brighter, and, therefore, visible farther, yet this is without fuel; and, I am persuaded no part of the electric fluid flies off in such case to distant places, but all goes directly, and is to be found in the place to which I destine it. May not different degrees of vibration of the above-mentioned universal medium occasion the appearances of different colours? I think the electric fluid is always the same, yet I find that weaker and stronger sparks differ in apparent colour; some white, blue, purple, red; the strongest, white; weak ones, red. Thus different degrees of vibration given to the air produce the 7 different sounds in music, analogous to the 7 colours, yet the medium, air, is the same.

If the sun is not wasted by expence of light, I can easily conceive that he shall otherwise always retain the same quantity of matter; tho' we should suppose him made of sulphur constantly flaming. The action of fire only *separates* the particles of matter; it does not *annihilate* them: water by heat rais'd in vapour, returns to the earth in rain. And if we could collect all the particles of burning matter that go off in smoke, perhaps they might, with the ashes, weigh as much as the body before it was fired; and, if we could put them into the same position with regard to each other, the mass would be the same as before, and might be burnt over again. The chemists have analys'd sulphur, and find it compos'd, in certain proportions, of oil, salt, and earth; and, having by the analysis discovered those proportions, they can, of those ingredients, make sulphur. So we have only to suppose, that the parts of the sun's sulphur, separated by fire rise into his atmosphere, there, being freed from the immediate action of the fire, they collect into cloudy masses, and growing by degrees too heavy to be longer supported, they descend to the sun, and are burnt over again. Hence the spots appearing on his face, which are observ'd to diminish daily in size, their consuming edges being of particular brightness.

It is well we are not, as poor Galileo was, subject to the Inquisition for philosophical heresy. My whispers against the orthodox doctrine, in private letters, would be dangerous; but your writing and printing would be highly criminal. As it is, you must expect some censure; but one heretic will surely excuse another.

I am heartily glad to hear more instances of the success of the poke-weed, in the cure of that horrible evil to the human body, a cancer. You will deserve highly of mankind for the communication. But I find in Boston they are at a loss to know the right plant, some asserting it is what they call *mechoacan*, others other things. In one of their late papers it is publickly requested, that a perfect description may be given of the plant, its places of growth, &c. I have mislaid the paper, or would send it to you. I tho't you had describ'd it pretty fully.

With great respect and esteem etc.

B. FRANKLIN.

QUERIES ON ELECTRICITY

From Dr. Ingenhousz; *with Answers*
by Dr. Franklin

[1780]

Question I

IF the electrical fluid is truly accumulated on the inside of a
Leyden phial, and expelled in the same proportion from
the other side, why are the particles of glass not all thrown
outwards, when the phial being overcharged breaks, or is perforated by a spontaneous explosion?

Answer

By the circumstances that have appeared to me, in all the
jarrs that I have seen perforated at the time of their explosion,
I have imagined that the charge did not pass by those perforations. Several single jarrs, that have broke while I was charging them, have shown, besides the perforation in the body, a
trace on both sides the neck, wherein the polish of the glass was
taken off the breadth of a straw; which prov'd that great part
at least of the charge, probably all, had passed over that trace. I
was once present at the discharge of a battery containing 30
jarrs, of which 8 were perforated and spoilt at the time of the
discharge; yet the effect of the charge on the bodies upon which
it was intended to operate, did not appear to be diminished. Another time I was present when twelve out of twenty jarrs were

broke at the time of the discharge; yet the effect of the charge, which pass'd in the regular circuit, was the same as it would have been if they had remained whole. Were those perforations an effect of the charge within the jarr forcing itself thro' the glass to get at the outside, other difficulties would arise and demand explanation. 1. How it happens, that in 8 bottles, and in 12, the strength to bear a strong charge should be so equal, that no one of them would break before the rest, and thereby save his fellows; but all should burst at the same instant. 2. How it happens, that they bear the force of the great charge till the instant that an easier means of discharge is offered them, which they make use of, and yet the fluid breaks thro' at the same time?

My conjecture is, that there has been, in the place where the rupture happens, some defect in the glass, some grain of sand perhaps, or some little bubble in the substance nearly void, where, during the charging of the jarr, the electric fluid is forc'd in and confin'd till the pressure is suddenly taken off by the discharge, when not being able to escape so quickly, it bursts its way out by its elastic force. Hence all the ruptures happen nearly at the same instant with the regular discharge, tho' really a little posterior, not being themselves discharges, but the effects of a discharge which pass'd in another channel.

Question II

When a strong explosion is directed thro' a pack of cards or a book, having a piece of tinfoil between several of its leaves, the electrical flash makes an impression on some of those metalic leaves, by which it seems as if the direction of the electric explosion had gone from the outside towards the inside, when, on the other metallic leaves, the impression is in such a direction, that it indicates the current of electrical fire to have made its way from the inside of the phial towards the outside; so that it appears to some electricians, that, in the time of the explosion of an electrical phial, two streams of electrical fire rush at the same time from both surfaces, and meet or cross one another.

Answer

These impressions are not effects of a moving body, striking with force in the direction of its motion; they are made by the burs rising in the neighbouring perforated cards, which rise accidentally, sometimes on one side of a card, sometimes on the other, in consequence of certain circumstances in the form of their surfaces or substances or situations. In a single card, supported without touching others, while perforated by the passing fluid, the bur generally rises on both sides, as I once show'd to Mr. Symmer at his house. I imagine that the hole is made by a fine thread of el. fluid first passing, and augmented to a bigger thread at the time of the explosion, which, obliging the parts of the card to recede every way, condenses a part within the substance, and forces a part out on each side, because there is least resistance.

.　　.　　.　　.　　.　　.　　.　　.　　.　　.

Question IV

Tho', from the very charging of the Leiden phial, it seems clear, that the electrical fluid does in reality not pervade the substance of glass, yet it is still difficult to conceive how such a subtil fluid may be forced out from one side of a very thick pane of glass, by a similar quantity of electrical fire thrown upon the other surface, and yet that it does not pass thro' any substance of glass, however thin, without breaking it. Is there some other fact or illustration besides those to be found in your public writings, by which it may be made more obvious to our understanding, that electrical fire does not enter at all the very substance of glass, and yet may force from the opposite surface an equal quantity; or that it enters really the pores of the glass without breaking it? Is there any comparative illustration or example in nature, by which it may be made clear, that a fluid thrown upon one surface of any body, may force out the same fluid from the other surface without passing through the substance?

Answer

That the electric fluid, by its repulsive nature, is capable of forcing portions of the same fluid out of bodies without entring them itself, appears from this experiment. Approach an isolated body with a rubb'd tube of a glass; the side next the tube will then be electrized negatively, the opposite positively. If a pair of cork balls hang from that opposite side, the electrical fluid forc'd out of the body will appear in those balls, causing them to diverge. Touch that opposite side, and you thereby take away the positive electricity. Then remove the tube, and you leave the body all in a negative state. Hence it appears, that the electric fluid appertaining to the glass tube did not enter the body, but retir'd with the tube, otherwise it would have supply'd the body with the electricity it had lost.

With regard to *powder magazines*, my idea is, that to prevent the mischief which might be occasion'd by the stones of their walls flying about in case of accidental explosion, they should be constructed in the ground; that the walls should be lin'd with lead, the floor lead, all ¼ inch thick, and the joints well solder'd; the cover copper, with a little scuttle to enter the whole, in the form of a canister for tea. If the edges of the cover-scuttle fall into a copper channel containing mercury, not the smallest particle of air or moisture can enter to the powder, even tho' the walls stood in water, or the whole was under water.

MAGNETISM *and the* THEORY *of the* EARTH

TO

JAMES BOWDOIN

Philada May 31, 1788.

DEAR SIR,

. . . .

OUR ancient correspondence used to have something philosophical in it. As you are now more free from public cares, and I expect to be so in a few months, why may we not resume that kind of correspondence? Our much regretted friend Winthrop once made me the compliment, that I was good at starting game for philosophers; let me try if I can start a little for you.

Has the question, how came the earth by its magnetism, ever been consider'd?

Is it likely that *iron ore* immediately existed when this globe was first form'd; or may it not rather be suppos'd a gradual production of time?

If the earth is at present magnetical in virtue of the masses of iron ore contain'd in it, might not some ages pass before it had magnetic polarity?

Since iron ore may exist without that polarity, and by being plac'd in certain circumstances may obtain it from an external cause, is it not possible that the earth received its magnetism from some such cause?

In short, may not a magnetic power exist throughout our system, perhaps thro' all systems, so that if men could make a voyage in the starry regions, a compass might be of use? And may not such universal magnetism, with its uniform direction be serviceable in keeping the diurnal revolution of a planet more steady to the same axis?

Lastly, as the poles of magnets may be changed by the presence of stronger magnets, might not, in ancient times, the near passing of some large comet, of greater magnetic power than this globe of ours, have been a means of changing its poles, and thereby wrecking and deranging its surface, placing in different regions the effect of centrifugal force, so as to raise the waters of the sea in some, while they were depress'd in others?

Let me add another question or two, not relating indeed to magnetism, but, however, to the theory of the earth.

Is not the finding of great quantities of shells and bones of animals (natural to hot climates) in the cold ones of our present world, some proof that its poles have been changed? Is not the supposition, that the poles have been changed, the easiest way of accounting for the deluge, by getting rid of the old difficulty how to dispose of its waters after it was over? Since, if the poles were again to be changed, and plac'd in the present equator, the sea would fall there about 15 miles in height, and rise as much in the present polar regions; and the effect would be proportionable, if the new poles were plac'd anywhere between the present and the equator.

Does not the apparent wrack of the surface of this globe thrown up into long ridges of mountains, with strata in various positions, make it probable, that its internal mass is a fluid; but a fluid so dense as to float the heaviest of our substances? Do we know the limit of condensation air is capable of? Supposing it to grow denser *within* the surface, in the same proportion nearly as it does *without*, at what depth may it be equal in density with gold?

Can we easily conceive how the strata of the earth could have been so derang'd, if it had not been a mere shell supported by a heavier fluid? Would not such a suppos'd internal fluid globe be immediately sensible of a change in the situation of the earth's axis, alter its form, and thereby burst the shell, and throw up parts of it above the rest? As if we would alter the position of the fluid contain'd in the shell of an egg, and place its longest diameter where the shortest now is, the shell must break; but would be much harder to break, if the whole internal substance were as solid and hard as the shell.

Might not a wave, by any means rais'd in this supposed internal ocean of extreamly dense fluid, raise in some degree, as it passes the present shell of incumbent earth, and break it in some places, as in earthquakes? And may not the progress of such wave, and the disorders it occasions among the solids of the shell, account for the rumbling sound being first heard at a distance, augmenting as it approaches, and gradually dying away as it proceeds? A circumstance observ'd by the inhabitants of South America in their last great earthquake, that noise coming from a place some degrees north of Lima, and being trac'd by enquiry quite down to Buenos Ayres, proceeded regularly from north to south at the rate of   Leagues per minute, as I was inform'd by a very ingenious Peruvian whom I met with at Paris.

I am ever, my very dear friend, yours most affectionately,

B. FRANKLIN.

[227]

NATURE OF LIGHTNING

TO

JAMES BOWDOIN

Philadelphia, January 24, 1752.

SIR,

. . . .

YOUR explication of the crooked direction of lightning appears to me both ingenious and solid. When we can account as satisfactorily for the electrification of clouds, I think that branch of natural philosophy will be nearly compleat.

The air, undoubtedly, obstructs the motion of the electric fluid. Dry air prevents the dissipation of an electric atmosphere, the denser the more, as in cold weather. I question whether such an atmosphere can be retained by a body *in vacuo*. A common electrical vial requires a non-electric communication from the wire to every part of the charged glass; otherwise, being dry and clean, and filled with air only, it charges slowly, and discharges gradually by sparks, without a shock; but, exhausted of air, the communication is so open and free between the inserted wire and surface of the glass, that it charges as readily, and shocks as smartly as if filled with water: and I doubt not, but that, in the experiment you propose, the sparks would not only be near strait *in vacuo*, but strike at a greater distance than in the open air, though perhaps there would not be a loud explosion. As soon as I have a little leisure, I will make the experiment, and send you the result.

My supposition, that the sea might possibly be the grand source of lightning, arose from the common observation of its luminous appearance in the night, on the least motion; an appearance never observed in fresh water. Then I knew, that the electric fluid may be pumped up out of the earth, by the friction of a glass globe, on a non-electric cushion; and that, notwithstanding the surprizing activity and swiftness of that fluid, and the non-electric communication between all parts of the cushion and the earth, yet quantities would be snatch'd up by the revolving surface of the globe, thrown on the prime conductor, and dissipated in air. How this was done, and why that subtile, active spirit did not immediately return again from the globe into some part or other of the cushion, and so into the earth, was difficult to conceive; but, whether from its being opposed by a current setting upwards to the cushion, or from whatever other cause, that it did not so return was an evident fact. Then I considered the separate particles of water as so many hard spherules, capable of touching the salt only in points, and imagined a particle of salt could therefore no more be wet by a particle of water, than a globe by a cushion; that there might therefore be such a friction between these originally constituent particles of salt and water, as in a sea of globes and cushions; that each particle of water on the surface might obtain, from the common mass, some particles of the universally diffused, much finer, and more subtil electric fluid, and, forming to itself an atmosphere of those particles, be repelled from the then generally electrified surface of the sea, and fly away with them into the air. I thought, too, that possibly the great mixture of particles electric *per se,* in the ocean water, might, in some degree, impede the swift motion and dissipation of the electric fluid through it to the shores, &c. But, having since found, that salt in the water of an electric vial does not lessen the shock; and having endeavored in vain to produce that luminous appearance from a mixture of salt and water agitated; and observed, that even the sea-water will not produce it after some hours standing in a bottle; I suspect it to proceed from some principle yet unknown to us (which I would gladly make some experiments to discover, if I lived near the sea), and I grow more doubtful of my former supposition, and more ready to allow weight to that objection (drawn from the activity of the electric fluid, and the readiness of water to conduct), which you have indeed stated with great strength and clearness.

In the mean time, before we part with this hypothesis, let us think what to substitute in its place, I have sometimes queried, whether the friction of the air, an electric *per se,* in violent winds, among trees, and against the surface of the earth, might not pump up, as so many glass globes, quantities of the electric fluid, which the rising vapours might receive from the air, and retain in the clouds they form? on which I should be glad to have your sentiments. An ingenious friend of mine supposes the land clouds more likely to be electrified than the sea clouds. I send his letter for your perusal, which please to return me.

I have wrote nothing lately on electricity, nor observed any thing new that is material, my time being much taken up with other affairs. Yesterday I discharged four jars through a fine wire, tied up between two strips of glass; the wire was in part melted, and the rest broke into small pieces, from half an inch long, to half a quarter of an inch. My globe raises the electric fire with greater ease, in much greater quantities, by the means of a wire extended from the cushion, to the iron pin of a pump-handle behind my house, which communicates by the pump-spear with the water in the well.

By this post I send to . . . who is curious in that way, some meteorological observations and conjectures, and desire him to communicate them to you, as they may afford you some amusement, and I know you will look over them with a candid eye. By throwing our occasional thoughts on paper, we more readily discover the defects of our opinions, or we digest them better, and find new arguments to support them. This I sometimes practice; but such pieces are fit only to be seen by friends.

I am, &c.

B. F[RANKLIN].

S O U N D

TO

OLIVER NEAVE

July 20, 1762.

DEAR SIR,

I HAVE perused your paper on sound, and would freely mention to you, as you desire it, every thing that appeared to me to need correction: but nothing of that kind occurs to me, unless it be, where you speak of the air as "the *best* medium for conveying sound." Perhaps this is speaking rather too positively, if there be, as I think there are, some other mediums that will convey it farther and more readily. It is a well-known experiment, that the scratching of a pin at one end of a long piece of timber, may be heard by an ear applied near the other end, though it could not be heard at the same distance through the air. And two stones being struck smartly together under water, the stroke may be heard at a greater distance by an ear also placed under water in the same river, than it can be heard through the air. I think I have heard it near a mile; how much farther it may be heard, I know not; but suppose a great deal farther, because the sound did not seem faint, as if at a distance, like distant sounds through air, but smart and strong; and as if present just at the ear. I wish you would repeat these experiments now you are upon the subject, and add your own observations. And if you were to repeat, with your naturally exact attention and observation, the common experiment of the bell in the exhausted receiver, possibly something new may occur to you, in considering,

1. Whether the experiment is not ambiguous; *i.e.* whether the gradual exhausting of the air, as it creates an increasing difference of pressure on the outside, may not occasion in the glass a difficulty of vibrating, that renders it less fit to communicate to the air without, the vibrations that strike it from within; and the diminution of the sound arise from this cause, rather than from the diminution of the air?

2. Whether as the particles of air themselves are at a distance from each other, there must not be some medium between them proper for conveying sound, since otherwise it would stop at the first particle?

3. Whether the great difference we experience in hearing sounds at a distance, when the wind blows towards us from the sonorous body, or towards that from us, can be well accounted for by adding to or subtracting from the swiftness of sound, the degree of swiftness that is in the wind at the time? The latter is so small in proportion, that it seems as if it could scarce produce any sensible effect, and yet the difference is very great. Does not this give some hint, as if there might be a subtile fluid, the conductor of sound, which moves at different times in different directions over the surface of the earth, and whose motion may perhaps be much swifter than that of the air in our strongest winds; and that in passing through air, it may communicate that motion to the air which we call wind, though a motion in no degree so swift as its own?

4. It is somewhere related, that a pistol fired on the top of

an exceeding high mountain, made a noise like thunder in the valleys below. Perhaps this fact is not exactly related; but if it is, would not one imagine from it, that the rarer the air, the greater sound might be produced in it from the same cause?

5. Those balls of fire which are sometimes seen passing over a country, computed by philosophers to be often 30 miles high at least, sometimes burst at that height; the air must be exceeding rare there, and yet the explosion produces a sound that is heard at that distance, and for 70 miles round on the surface of the earth, so violent too as to shake buildings, and give an apprehension of an earthquake. Does not this look as if a rare atmosphere, almost a vacuum, was no bad conductor of sound?

I have not made up my mind on these points, and only mention them for your consideration, knowing that every subject is the better for your handling it.

With the greatest esteem, I am, &c.

B. FRANKLIN.

PREHISTORIC ANIMALS
of the OHIO

TO

ABBÉ CHAPPE

London, Jan. 31. 1768

SIR

I SENT you sometime since, directed to the care of M. Molini, a bookseller near the Quay des Augustins a tooth that I mention'd to you when I had the pleasure of meeting with you at the Marquis de Courtanvaux's. It was found near the River Ohio in America, about 200 leagues below Fort du Quesne, at what is called the Great Licking Place, where the earth has a saltish taste that is agreable to the buffaloes & deer, who come there at certain seasons in great numbers to lick the same. At this place have been found the skeletons of near 30 large animals suppos'd to be elephants, several tusks like those of elephants, being found with these grinder teeth—four of these grinders were sent me by the gentleman who brought them from the Ohio to New York, together with 4 tusks, one of which is 6 feet long & in the thickest part near 6 inches diameter, and also one of the vertebrae—My Lord Shelbourn receiv'd at the same time 3 or four of them with a jaw bone & one or two grinders remaining in it. Some of our naturalists here, however, contend, that these are not the grinders of elephants

[235]

but of some carnivorous animal unknown, because such knobs
or prominences on the face of the tooth are not to be found on
those of elephants, and only, as they say, on those of carnivorous animals. But it appears to me that animals capable of
carrying such large & heavy tusks, must themselves be large
creatures, too bulky to have the activity necessary for pursuing
and taking prey; and therefore I am inclin'd to think those
knobs are only a small variety, animals of the same kind and
name often differing more materially, and that those knobs
might be as useful to grind the small branches of trees, as to
chaw flesh—However I should be glad to have your opinion,
and to know from you whether any of the kind have been found
in Siberia.

With great esteem & respect, I am

      Sir

           Your most obed^t hum^l Servant

               B.F.

TOADS FOUND IN STONE

A T Passy, near Paris, April 6, 1782, being with M. de
Chaumont, viewing his quarry, he mention'd to me,
that the workmen had found a living toad shut up in
the stone. On questioning one of them, he told us, they had
found four in different cells which had no communication; that
they were very lively and active when set at liberty; that there
was in each cell some loose, soft, yellowish earth, which appeared to be very moist. We asked, if he could show us the parts
of the stone that form'd the cells. He said, No; for they were
thrown among the rest of what was dug out, and he knew not
where to find them. We asked, if there appear'd any opening
by which the animal could enter. He said, No. We asked, if in
the course of his business as a labourer in quarries, he had often
met with the like. He said, Never before. We asked, if he could
show us the toads. He said, he had thrown two of them up on
a higher part of the quarry, but knew not what became of the
others.

He then came up to the place where he had thrown the two,
and, finding them, he took them by the foot, and threw them
up to us, upon the ground where we stood. One of them was
quite dead, and appear'd very lean; the other was plump and
still living. The part of the rock where they were found, is at
least fifteen feet below its surface, and is a kind of limestone. A
part of it is filled with ancient sea-shells, and other marine substances. If these animals have remain'd in that confinement
since the formation of the rock, they are probably some thou-

sands of years old. We have put them in spirits of wine, to preserve their bodies a little longer. The workmen have promis'd to call us, if they meet with any more, that we may examine their situation. Before a suitable bottle could be found to receive them, that which was living when we first had them appeared to be quite dead and motionless; but being in the bottle, and spirits pour'd over them, he flounced about in it very vigorously for two or three minutes, and then expir'd.

It is observed, that animals who perspire but little, can live long without food; such as tortoises, whose flesh is cover'd with [a thick shell, and snakes, who are covered with] scales, which are of so close a substance as scarcely to admit the passage of perspirable matter thro' them. Animals that have open pores all over the surface of their bodies, and live in air which takes off continually the perspirable part of their substance, naturally require a continual supply of food to maintain their bulk. Toads shut up in solid stone, which prevents their losing any thing of their substance, may perhaps for that reason need no supply; and being guarded against all accidents, and all the inclemencies of the air and changes of the seasons, are, it seems, subject to no diseases, and become as it were immortal.

B. FRANKLIN.

LETTERS *and* PAPERS *in this* VOLUME

Original manuscripts or early printings are to be found as indicated:

A.P.S.	American Philosophical Society
D.S.	State Department, Washington
Dub. F.	Barbeu Dubourg's *Oeuvres de M. Franklin* (1773)
E. & O.	Franklin's *Experiments and Observations on Electricity* (London, 1769)
L.C.	Library of Congress
Ros.	The Rosenbach Company
Sp.	Jared Sparks' *The Works of Benjamin Franklin*, 10 volumes
U. of Pa.	Library of the University of Pennsylvania
W. S. M.	William Smith Mason's Collection

PRACTICAL SCHEMES AND SUGGESTIONS

To the Authors of the Journal of Paris [1784]

To Barbeu Dubourg, London, July 28, 1768 (*Dub. F. II, 310*)

To Alexander Small, Passy, July 22, 1780 (*see "Private Corres. of B. Franklin"* (*1818*), *I, 64*)

To John Pringle, London, December 21, 1757 (*E. & O. 359*)

To Benjamin Vaughan, Philadelphia, July 31, 1786 (*L.C.*)

Rules of Health and Long Life, *Poor Richard's Almanack*, 1742

The Art of Procuring Pleasant Dreams [1786] (*Sp. II, 171*)

To Barbeu Dubourg [1773] (*Dub. F. II, 258*)

To Oliver Neave, date unknown (*Dub. F. II, 241*)

To Mrs. Jane Mecom, London, July 17, 1771 (*Ros.*)

To George Whatley, Passy, May 23, 1785 (*L.C.*)

Of Lightning, and the method (now used in America) of securing buildings and persons from its mischievous effects, Paris, September, 1767 (*E. & O. 579*)

To —— —— [1772 ?] (*A.P.S.*) (*Franklin Papers, XLVI, Part 1, 30*)

An Account of the New-Invented Pennsylvanian Fire-Places, 1744

To Barbeu Dubourg and Thomas François Dalibard [1773] (*Dub. F. I, 327*)

To S. Rhoads, London, August 22, 1772 (*W. S. M.*)

Indian Corn, date unknown (*L.C.*)

To Giambatista Beccaria, London, July 13, 1762 (*Sp. VI, 245*)

DIVERS EXPERIMENTS AND OBSERVATIONS

To Sir Joseph Banks, Passy, August 30, 1783 (*U. of Pa.*)

To Sir Joseph Banks, Passy, October 8, 1783 (*U. of Pa.*)

To Sir Joseph Banks, Passy, November 21, 1783 (*U. of Pa.*)

To Sir Joseph Banks, Passy, December 1, 1783 (*see A. L. Rotch, in Proceedings of the American Antiquarian Society, XVIII*)

To Jan Ingenhousz, Passy, January 16, 1784 (*L.C.*)

To Peter Collinson [c. 1750] (*E. & O. 350*)

To Peter Collinson [Philadelphia], 1748 (*E. & O. 21*)

To John Lining, Philadelphia, March 18, 1755 (*E. & O. 319*)

To Peter Collinson [Philadelphia], October 19, 1752 (*E. & O. 111*)

To —— ——, Philadelphia, July 12, 1753 (*A.P.S.*) (*Franklin Papers, L, Part 1, 37*)

To Thomas Ronayne, London, April 20, 1766 (*Dub. F. I, 265*)

To Lord Kames, London, June 2, 1765 (*see Memoirs of the Life & Writings of the Honourable Henry Home of Kames, II, 16*)

To David Le Roy, At sea, August, 1785 (*see "Transactions of the American Philosophical Society," II, 294*)

To Anthony Todd, London, October 29, 1769 (*Public Record Office, London*)

To Sir John Pringle, London, May 10, 1768 (*E. & O. 492*)

To Mary Stevenson, London, August 10, 1761 (*Sp. VI, 232*)

To John Pringle, Philadelphia, December 1, 1762 (*E. & O. 438*)

To Joseph Priestley, London, April 10, 1774 (*see Priestley's "Experiments on Air," 3rd ed., I, 321*)

To Mrs. Jane Mecom, Philadelphia, June 19, 1731 (*see Sparks' "A Collection of the Familiar Letters of Benjamin Franklin"*)

To Barbeu Dubourg [1773] (*Dub. F. I, 327*)

SCIENTIFIC DEDUCTIONS AND CONJECTURES

To Benjamin Rush, London, July 14, 1773 (*D.S.*)
Definition of a Cold [1773] (*L.C.*)
To John Lining, New York, April 14, 1757 (*Sp. VI, 203*)
To John Lining, London, June 17, 1758 (*E. & O. 363*)
To Jared Eliot, Philadelphia, July 16, 1747 (*Yale University*)
To Mary Stevenson, London, September 13, 1760 (*Sp. VI, 225*)
To Mary Stevenson [September 20, 1761] (*Sp. VI, 234*)
To Peter Franklin, London, May 7, 1760 (*E. & O. 379*)
To Alexander Small, May 12, 1760 (*E. & O. 381*)
To William Brownrigg, London, November 7, 1773 (*see "Philosophical Transactions," LXIV, 445*)
To John Perkins, Philadelphia, February 4, 1753 (*A.P.S.*)
To Humphry Marshall, London, February 14, 1773 (*D.S.*)
To Cadwallader Colden, Philadelphia, April 23, 1752 (*A.P.S.*)
Queries on Electricity from Dr. Ingenhousz; with Answers by Dr. Franklin [1780] (*L.C.*)
To James Bowdoin, Philadelphia, May 31, 1788 (*L.C.*)
To James Bowdoin, Philadelphia, January 24, 1752 (*E. & O. 173*)
To Oliver Neave, July 20, 1762 (*E. & O. 435*)
To Abbé Chappe, London, January 31, 1768 (*A.P.S.*)
Toads Found in Solid Stone [1782] (*L.C.*)

CORRESPONDENTS MENTIONED *in* *this* VOLUME

Banks, Sir Joseph, English naturalist; President of the Royal Society
Beccaria, Giambatista, Italian astronomer and physicist
Bowdoin, James, American statesman
Brownrigg, William, English physician and chemist
Chappe d'Auteroche, Abbé, French astronomer
Colden, Cadwallader, English botanist and physician in America
Collinson, Peter, English naturalist and antiquarian
Dalibard, Thomas Francis, French botanist and natural philosopher
Dubourg, Barbeu, French physician and botanist
Eliot, Jared, New England clergyman and agriculturist
Franklin, Peter, Benjamin Franklin's brother
Ingenhousz, Jan, Dutch physician and physicist
Kames, Lord (Henry Home), Scottish judge and author
Le Roy, Julien David, French architect
Lining, John, American physician
Marshall, Humphry, American botanist
Mecom, Mrs. Jane, Benjamin Franklin's sister
Neave, Oliver, Anglo-American merchant
Perkins, John, Boston physician
Priestley, Joseph, English theologian and scientist
Pringle, Sir John, English physician
Rhoads, Samuel, Member of Pennsylvania Assembly, Mayor of Philadelphia
Ronayne, Thomas, physicist and glass manufacturer at Cork, Ireland
Rush, Benjamin, American physician
Small, Alexander, British army surgeon
Stevenson, Mary, daughter of the landlady of Franklin's London residence
Todd, Anthony, Secretary of the British General Post-Office
Vaughan, Benjamin, English politician
Whatley, George, English economist

A FEW ADDITIONAL LETTERS *and* PAPERS *of* INTEREST *to the* GENERAL READER

(References are to Albert Henry Smyth's edition of *The Writings of Benjamin Franklin*, 10 volumes, New York, 1905–7)

To Josiah and Abiah Franklin, On Smallpox and Cancer, Philadelphia, September 6, 1774 (*Smyth II, 281*)

To Dr. John Hawkesworth, Treatment for Cancer, May 8, 1772 (*X, 279*)

To Thomas Percival, Moist Air and Health, West Wycomb, September 25, 1773 (*VI, 138*)

To Jean Baptiste Le Roy, Perspiration, London, June 22, 1773 (*VI, 59*)

To Barbeu Dubourg, Colds, March 10, 1773 (*VI, 26*)

To Barbeu Dubourg, Colds, London, June 29, 1773 (*VI, 61*)

To Cadwallader Evans, Lead Poisoning, London, February 20, 1768 (*V, 101*)

To Jan Ingenhousz, Air and Health, At sea, August 28, 1785 (*IX, 413*)

To Peter Collinson, First Electrical Experiments, July 11, 1747 (*II, 302*)

To Peter Collinson, First Electrical Experiments, September 1, 1747 (*II, 325*)

Opinions and Conjectures, Concerning the Properties and Effects of the Electrical Matter, Arising from Experiments and Observations, made at Philadelphia, 1749 (*II, 427*) Single Fluid Theory of Electricity.

To Peter Collinson, Various Electrical Experiments, June 27, 1750 (*II, 423*)

To Peter Collinson, Electrical Nature of Clouds, Philadelphia, September, 1753 (*III, 148*)

To Barbeu Dubourg, The Magnetic Field, London, March 10, 1773 (*VI, 23*)

To Barbeu Dubourg, Influence of Electricity on Glass, London, June 1, 1773 (*VI, 52*)

[243]